Beverley Nichols

THE FOOL HATH SAID

Other books by
BEVERLEY NICHOLS

THE
FOOL HATH SAID

by

BEVERLEY NICHOLS

The fool hath said in his heart,
There is no God

JONATHAN CAPE
THIRTY BEDFORD SQUARE
LONDON

FIRST PUBLISHED 1936

JONATHAN CAPE LTD.   30 BEDFORD SQUARE, LONDON
AND 91 WELLINGTON STREET WEST, TORONTO

PRINTED IN GREAT BRITAIN IN THE CITY OF OXFORD
AT THE ALDEN PRESS
PAPER MADE BY JOHN DICKINSON & CO., LTD.
BOUND BY A. W. BAIN & CO., LTD.

CONTENTS

PART I

PART II

To
M. E. I. G.

PART I

THIS LITTLE UNIVERSE

I

I WANT you to regard the first part of this book as a treasure hunt rather than as a theological essay.

Not that I have anything against theological essays. Indeed, many of them are wildly exciting. They are like celestial jig-saw puzzles in which slowly, piece by piece, the pattern comes into view — till you put the last fragment in, when the whole design turns to gold. And you wonder why you have taken so long over such a simple design, such a very ordinary design. A common cross.

The treasure we are seeking is Faith.

Before that confession makes you throw this book away may I very hastily, tugging at your sleeve, make three brief observations:

Firstly, I do not see why such a treasure hunt should deprive us of our sense of humour. Christ was, after all, by far the greatest wit that the world has ever known. Most men's epigrams are like sparks — they fly up into contemporary skies, light up a tiny fragment of landscape, put out an eye, and then they are as ashes. But Christ's epigrams are like stars. And like the stars, they are as near to eternity as we could want. Consider, for example, that extremely startling statement (which was not saved up for a dinner table, but was casually thrown off in a conversation with some fishermen) — *For he that hath, to him shall be given: and he that hath not, from him shall be taken even that which he hath.* If Christ had said only that one sentence he would have said more than most men in their passage through this world. For this sentence is not only an epigram, and not only a shrewd criticism of the process of contemporary capitalist society. It is also, as Aldous Huxley has pointed out, the formulation of a natural law. Indeed, it might very well have served as a text on the front page of the *Origin of Species*. I often wonder if Darwin conveniently forgot it when he wrote his famous passage about being unable to reconcile the existence of a beneficent God with the existence of the Ichneumonidae.

Secondly, still tugging at your sleeve, I should like to observe that there is no reason why we should not employ, in this book, all the battery of scientific apparatus which is so dear to the heart of the modern detective story writer, the microscope, the searchlight, the telescope, the calligraphy expert, and all that.

It would be unfair, at this point, to suggest where these inquiries will lead us. But they *must* be used, because I have no use for Faith that is not based on Fact.

Christianity is either History or it is nothing. At least, that is how the average modern man feels about it. We can respect, even envy, those many fine souls who have only to fall on their knees to see a revelation of the divine truth. Nor need we deny the authenticity of their revelation. Spiritual things, as Saint Paul said, are spiritually discerned. But you and I, at the outset, are not relying on inspiration. We want the evidence of a Court of Law, with the fullest privilege of cross-examination.

And now we come to the third observation. If you will listen to this, I believe that there will no longer be any reason to tug at your sleeve. For the third thing I want to say is about the Treasure itself.

Whatever else you may say about it, you can hardly deny that IF it were obtainable it would be worth a great deal more than anything else that this world could possibly offer. It may seem odd to quote an eminent sceptic like Aldous Huxley twice in the first two pages of a book on religion, but I cannot help being reminded of a passage in one of his most charming essays, called 'Wanted, A New Pleasure'. Here he says:

'So far as I can see, the only possible new pleasure would be one derived from the invention of a new drug — of a more efficient and less harmful substitute for alcohol and cocaine. If I were a millionaire, I should endow a band of research workers to look for the ideal intoxicant. If we could sniff or swallow something that would abolish our solitude as individuals, atone us with our fellows in a glowing exaltation of affection and make life in all its aspects seem not only worth living, but divinely beautiful and significant, and if this heavenly, world-transfiguring drug were of such a kind that we could wake up next morning with a clear head and an undamaged constitution — then, it seems to me, all our problems would be wholly solved and earth would become paradise.'

Well, some people have this thing. Huxley calls it a 'drug'. They call it Faith. And whatever else Huxley may say about it, he cannot possibly deny that it works. Apply his own tests:

'Abolish our solitude as individuals.'

'Atone us with our fellows in a glowing exaltation.'

'Make life in all its aspects seem not only worth living but divinely beautiful and significant.'

'Of such a kind that we could wake up next morning with a clear head and an undamaged constitution.'

Huxley, as we have observed before, cannot deny that all these phenomena are induced by the 'drug' — his word, not mine — called Faith. And to this list of blessings we can add a great many more. The drug is, for example, a talisman which abolishes all economic inequalities. A single dose of it, and you have the same income as Mr. Pierpont Morgan, invested in securities which are not subject to the fluctuations of any worldly market. A single dose of it and you are eternally young — as young as the Sons of the Morning. A single dose of it, and you have abolished the great phantom that stands in the way of all human happiness, the phantom of Fear. For if none of us were afraid, the world would be a golden place — yes, if none of us were afraid of losing that which we have, whether it be an earthy treasure or a spiritual, a garden, or a smile, or the rhythm of our own hearts, keeping in time with the clocks of this world.

The only thing to which Huxley can legitimately object in Faith is that it is a drug which does not 'take' on certain constitutions. He may, or may not, regret this. However, he should remember that in a very large number of cases where the drug does not 'take', the reason for its failure is that the unsuccessful patients have not followed the directions of the Chief Physician. Those directions were of the utmost simplicity. Christ said

'Knock and it shall be opened unto you'. If you ignore those directions you might as well complain that a medicine would not do you any good when all the time you had omitted to carry out the very simple suggestion that you should shake the bottle.

Most people try to take the 'drug' standing up, walking about, talking, fussing. It is a pity that they did not do as they were told, and fall on their knees, in a quiet room.

II

Now, if we are going to start out on this hunt together, it will be best if we assume, at the outset, that we don't believe anything at all. We have no preconceived ideas. All we know, for a very definite fact, is that certain people *have* discovered a treasure which, from all available evidence, makes them supremely happy, acts as an ano-dyne in pain, a comforter in solitude, and an unfailing remedy for every possible sort of depression. These persons, in all other respects, appear to be sane. They do not perpetually froth at the mouth, nor rush about under the impression that they are the local Joan of Arc. They seem, on the contrary, extremely normal.

It is obviously worth an hour or two's search to see if we can possibly share this blessing with them.

But here at the outset, we have a hurdle to surmount. It is a very considerable hurdle. In fact it is the Universe.

The Universe has a tactless way of obtruding itself upon the consciousness of even the best-intentioned of us. We start off for church, and on the way we see the

Universe at work, in the shape of a cat playing with a mouse. We try to get the mouse away, perhaps we succeed, and we perform the extremely distasteful task of stamping on the little mauled thing to put it out of its pain. Then, illogically, we stroke the cat, which 'doesn't know any better'. But why doesn't it know any better? That is the question which keeps cropping up, even through the Psalms:

'*O give thanks unto the Lord; for he is good . . .*'

Yes, but he put the mouse into the cat's paws.

'*For his mercy endureth for ever . . .*'

Perhaps there are a million mice in a million cats' paws at this very moment.

'*To him that by wisdom made the heavens . . .*'

Will mice go to heaven?

'*That stretched out the earth above the waters . . .*'

And the claw above the mouse.

And so it goes on. The whole service is spoilt. It looks as though Faith is indeed a 'drug', if we have to forget even this minor instance of the bestiality of the Universe in order to believe in a loving God.

It is significant that Darwin, in the before mentioned passage on the Ichneumonidae, was also worried by the thought of the cat and the mouse. And yet, in that very same passage, he ended up by saying, 'I feel most deeply that the whole subject is too profound for human speculation. A dog might as well speculate on the mind of Newton'.

And when some years later, Tennyson asked him if his theory of Evolution made against Christianity, Darwin replied, very emphatically, 'Certainly not'.

So, perhaps, Darwin still leaves the church door open. Not very far open, we must admit. And there is a shadow of a cat across the porch. And a lot of other shadows as well. Perhaps the people who are coming out of the door, with such radiant faces, do not see the shadows? Or perhaps they have a secret which makes them see more clearly? It must be a pretty wonderful secret if it makes them see more clearly than a man like Darwin.

Well, perhaps it is.

III

So far, our little leap at this awkward preliminary hurdle of the Universe has not met with any marked success. All we did was to trip over a cat, land on our faces, and see stars.

And as we stare up through the hurdle, to the sky, where we are told the treasure is hid, we go on seeing stars. An almost vulgar number of stars. There they are, in the heavens, like diamond dust, twinkling with cold detachment. For all we know there are millions of cats and millions of mice on those stars, indulging in cruelty to the nth degree, through all eternity. For all we know the heavens are merely an immense arena created for the delectation of an arch-Sadist. There may be, to parody Sir James Jeans, cats in those stars which first caught a mouse in the reign of Charles I, and have gone on chasing it ever since. Pain may be eternal, remorseless. The degree of the agony may be commensurate with the size of the stage.

We are up against the Universe with a vengeance now. It sweeps down on us, like the lid of a coffin, and every star is a nail, a glittering nail driven in by a master-hand to emphasize the blackness of our night.

Of what use, in moments like these, to remember the feeble little words of Christ, 'Let not your heart be troubled, neither let it be afraid'?

And yet, somehow, even as we say them, they do not sound feeble. Nor little. Nor — in some curious way — do they sound *false*. They ring down the centuries, like a distant bell, that you can hear pealing even on a night of storm and terror.

We look up to the stars again. They do not seem quite as formidable as they were. Indeed, for a moment we could almost believe, with the painters of the Renaissance, that they were only golden toys, hung by God on the celestial tree to give His children pleasure, and to light their feet by night.

Which brings me, somewhat reluctantly, to a fragment of autobiography.

IV

I was 'confirmed' by the Bishop of Salisbury, at Marlborough College in — I think — the year 1916. In spite of all that you or I may say against public school religion, the ceremony was a very beautiful one, of the utmost spiritual value to a sensitive boy in the cloudy and distressful April of adolescence. In some ways I wish it had not been so beautiful. For it made the subsequent awakening all the more bitter.

The awakening was administered by Shelley. Shelley and his damned stars. Those same stars which, under the influence of Sir James Jeans and other popular astronomers, are blinding so many people to-day in the name of 'science'.

One day, shortly after confirmation, I escaped from a very dull cricket match, and departed to the library, intent on the exciting game of 'seeing how it was done'. By this, I mean, that I pored over endless notes, criticisms and theories of literature which 'showed the works'. A peculiar form of perversity made me much more interested in the actual methods by which a poem had been constructed than in the poem itself. Never shall I forget the thrill with which I encountered a photograph of the manuscript of *L'Allegro*, showing the very large number of corrections and emendations to which Milton had subjected it. Perhaps the most entrancing discovery of all was Poe's essay on 'The Rationale of Verse', in which each stage in the manufacture of *The Raven* is shown us as clearly as if he were building up an engine from the first screw to the last.

I was now on the trail of Shelley. How had that music come to him? Easily — rapturously, or with pain? 'Hail to thee, blithe spirit!' Had he written those words spontaneously, or had he first paid the skylark some other tribute less exquisitely appropriate than 'blithe'? Eagerly I reached for the lyrics and shorter poems of Percy Bysshe Shelley, found a quiet corner, and sat down to read.

When I began to read it was a glorious afternoon. The sun poured down on the open pages. In the light of after events it seems symbolical that as I read on, the clouds began to gather outside, and darkness swept over the building, and a roll of thunder. Before I had finished, I had to turn on the lamp. I stayed there, bent on those pages in a sort of horrified, guilty fascination.

In some ways I wish I had never turned on the lamp. For I had opened the pages at Shelley's 'Notes to Queen Mab'.

V

One of the difficulties that some men find with entirely orthodox Christianity is the doctrine of the Atonement. They cannot see why babies are 'born in sin'. Sin, one would have thought, was intentional. What does a little child, blinking at the sunlight, know about it? And I must confess that to me sin has always meant a sin against beauty, in some form or other — it has meant the first tarnish on the mirror, the first ugly line round a young mouth, the first bruised petal of a spray of blossom. And the hideous thing, which all adult people should remember, is that it is nearly always *we* who cause the tarnish or the ugly lines or the bruised petals. It is part of our own damnable corruption, which we cannot keep to ourselves.

All of which, you may say, has nothing to do with the 'Notes to Queen Mab'. Yet it has. For if ever a boy was corrupted by a book, I was corrupted. It was as though Shelley, who had enchanted me with his gay singing, had suddenly burst into an obscene cackle of laughter. On and on went the laughter, echoing in my brain, chasing away the skylark from his own heaven, sending his aerie spirits affrighted, making a mockery of his 'music when sweet voices die', blasting with its bitter breath the flowers he had laid on the tomb of Adonais. Shelley, who had created a universe of beauty for me, suddenly destroyed it with a clap of his hands.

In a moment we will see what Shelley said in those notes. But first I should explain that it was because I was very young, and because Shelley was my particular hero, that his words meant so much to me. An older boy can do almost anything he likes with a younger boy who worships him, can twist him to any mould, fine or base. And Shelley, at that time, could do almost anything with me. For it was Shelley who had written

> To that high Capital, where kingly Death
> Keeps his pale court in beauty and decay,
> He came; and bought with price of purest breath,
> A grave among the eternal ...

You do not argue with men from whose lips such words are dropped. You do not, you dare not, even speak to them. You can only close your eyes, and thank God for their existence.

Thank God!

But how could I thank God, when there was no God to thank? When Shelley himself told me there was no God to thank? For this was the first note on which my eyes had fallen:

'There is no God.'

The plurality of worlds — the indefinite immensity of the universe is a most awful subject of contemplation. He who rightly feels its mystery and grandeur is in no danger of seduction from the falsehoods of religious systems, or of deifying the principle of the universe. It is impossible to believe that the Spirit that pervades this infinite machine begat a son upon the body of a Jewish woman; or is angered at the consequences of that necessity, which is a synonym of itself. All that miserable tale of the Devil, and Eve, and an Intercessor, with the childish mummeries of the God of the Jews, is irreconcilable with the knowledge of the stars. The works of His fingers have borne witness against Him.

'Immensity of the universe' . . . 'impossible to believe' . . . 'body of a Jewish woman' . . . 'childish mummeries of the God of the Jews'.

I read on. The storm outside gathered fresh violence. I remember wondering, in a confused sort of way, if the lightning would strike me dead.

VI

And that, I trust, will be the last fragment of auto-biography with which I need trouble you in these pages. It was, however, a necessary fragment, not only to give you a sketch, however shadowy, of my personal background in these matters, but also to face, once again, this question of the universe which is still, you may remember, the first hurdle we have to take before we can set out on the Treasure hunt.

The universe floored Shelley. Knocked him out. Made him see stars. Made him write that 'Sirius is supposed to be at least 54,224,000,000,000 miles from the earth'. It is difficult to think of those thin white fingers, which had celebrated the silver choiring of the skylark, bothering with such a big number as 54,224,000,000,000. But he was always bothering with numbers in these notes. He had taken a draught of the fiery spirits of Science, he who 'on honey dew had fed'. And quite naturally it had gone to his head.

Here are some of the lines of his tirade:

'God made man such as he is, and then damned him for being so.'

'War, imprisonment, assassination and falsehood, deeds of unexampled and incomparable atrocity, these have made Christianity what it is.'

'Prayer may be considered under two points of view: as an endeavour to change the intentions of God or as a formal testimony of our obedience.'

'If God is the author of good, he is also the author of evil; if he is entitled to our gratitude for the one, he is entitled to our hatred for the other.'

If only somebody a little wiser than Shelley had been looking over my shoulder! If only, even, there had been an older boy to point out that Shelley's definition of prayer might sound very well in the Lower Fourth but was not the sort of thing you would expect from a member of the Upper Sixth. Prayer is not 'an endeavour to change the intentions of God'. Rather is it an effort to find out what God's intentions are. However that is a subject which we will leave to a later chapter.

The main point, to which we must revert, is that

Shelley was frightened by the *size* of the universe. You can almost see his pen tremble as he writes, 'That which appears only a thin and silvery cloud streaking the heaven is in effect composed of innumerable clusters of suns, each shining with its own light, and illuminating numbers of planets that revolve around them'.

He is like a little country boy who is suddenly lost in New York. He looks up at the millions of windows, glaring at each other with arrogant inhumanity, he is jostled by the dense crowds on the side-walks, deafened by the screeching of motor-horns. He gropes feebly for some friendly hand. There is nobody. He has lost his way. He begins to cry. Poor little boy! Poor little Shelley!

VII

'How can God — if there be a God — conceivably take any special and particular interest in this peculiarly insignificant planet?'

'If this earth is only a grain of sand on an apparently limitless shore, is it, to say the least of it, *probable*, that our particular grain of sand should have been chosen out of the unthinkable number of billions? And is it, again, probable (let alone certain) that, in Shelley's words, the moving Spirit should have "begat a son upon the body of a Jewish woman"?'

These are the questions the average man has to answer. It is vitally important that he should answer them. And in order that there may be no shirking of the issue, no comforting, vague assurances of 'all being for the best', and 'not bothering about things we don't understand', let us go a step further than Shelley and turn to that popular work, *The Universe Around Us*, by Sir James Jeans. In this we read:

'There are thousands of millions of millions of stars within the range covered by the 100-inch telescope, and this number must be further multiplied to allow for the parts of the universe which are still unexplored. At a moderate computation the total number of stars in the universe must be something like the total number of specks of dust in London. Think of the sun as something less than a millionth part of a speck of dust in a vast city, of the earth as less than a millionth part of such a speck of dust, and we have perhaps as vivid a picture as the mind can really grasp of the relation of our home in space to the rest of the universe.'[1]

Our 'home' in space. It sounds a rather draughty sort of home, at first sight.

VIII

And yet I called this chapter 'Our *Little* Universe'. I gave it that title, not through any desire to be 'clever', or to make a cheap sensation, but because, after mature consideration, it seemed the best summary of the conclusions of the scientists themselves.

In a moment I hope to be able to show you (on the

[1] *The Universe Around Us*, pp. 86, 87.

authority of the same scientists who have so bewildered us) that all this talk about millions and billions and trillions is a little beside the point. Not that they do not exist, but that they are not really nearly so important as they sound. They are rather like the noughts at the end of our various national debts. If you added up all those noughts you would find that they represented a great deal more money than there is, ever has been, or ever could be, in the world. These noughts represent something called 'Credit', which is a bastard edition of Faith. It is odd that everybody believes in Credit (whose material foundations can be exploded by an intelligent child on half a sheet of note-paper) while very few believe in Faith. However that is by the way.

But before we puff away some of these long rows of noughts, I would like to register a polite astonishment at the fact that nobody seems to have drawn, from the facts which we are about to quote, the really amazing deductions which we *must* draw from them.

Below you will find four statements, by four of the most eminent modern scientists, which, in a few words, rob the universe of its terror, obliterate the bogy of 'Immensity' and re-establish this apparently insignificant earth in a position of paramount importance. These statements have been made *en plein air*, without any attempt at disguising them. And yet, with one exception, nobody seems to have noticed them. The exception is a very excellent little book in which they are mentioned together,[1] but even in this their world-shattering importance does not seem to have been grasped. World-

[1] *The Truth of Christianity*, Turton (Wells, Gardner, Darton and Co.).

shattering is not an exaggerated adjective. It is a literal summary of the substance of these men's conclusions — which are, to waste no more time:

'*That this earth, this speck of dust,* HAS *been chosen out of the infinite number of millions for a unique and particular purpose.*'

And now let us quote our authorities for this statement.

Here is what Sir Ambrose Fleming says about it:

Sir Ambrose Fleming: 'There is strong reason for believing that a planetary system like our own is very rare, if not *unique*, in the universe, and the nature and conditions of our earth unique amidst that uniqueness.'[1]

Well? That is a statement which, at least, gives one to think, does it not? Of course, he may be wrong, but still, if you look up Sir Ambrose in *Who's Who*, you will find that he is not without his qualifications. However, we will turn to a scientist of even greater eminence — Sir Arthur Eddington.

Sir Arthur Eddington: '*Not one* of the vast profusion of stars in their myriad clusters looks down on scenes comparable to those which are passing beneath the rays of our sun.'[2]

Well, again? This little grain of sand, the earth, which we had been inclined to hold in such contempt, begins to assume a particular sparkle of its own, does it not?

---

[1] Sir Ambrose Fleming, *Transactions of Victoria Institute.* Vol. lxv, p. 16, 1933.
[2] Sir Arthur Eddington, *Nature of Physical Universe,* p. 178. 1929.

It may not be very large, but if we are to trust the men who ought to know, there appears to be *something* rather different about it. Even if it is a pebble, it is a rather valuable sort of pebble, and we should be justified in collecting examples of it.

But, here's the point. We couldn't collect examples. Because it happens to be the only pebble. It seems impossible to believe. And yet — here is Sir Arthur Thomson, who ought to know something about these matters, confessing:

Sir Arthur Thomson: 'There is something awesome in the apparent uniqueness of our earth.'[1]

Unique! Again that word.

And you will find it, once more, in the pages of the same Sir James Jeans who has so greatly bewildered us. For in spite of all his millions and trillions, he too, agrees, that this little speck of dust is 'unique'.

Now, do you agree — for a moment at any rate, before your critical faculties begin to worry and bother again — that perhaps the painters, in the age of faith, were not such fools after all? To them the stars were a gay pattern, a spray of golden blossom glistening on Night's branches, a necklace hung round the sky's lovely throat. To them, the stars were as jewels on the robes of God — or, if you will, they were tiny windows through which a man might see shining the infinite glory of the grace beyond. That is how the stars were in the age of Faith, when, as Browning said, 'reds were reds, and blues were blues', and when the gold with which they scattered the skies of their

[1] Sir Arthur Thomson, *Purpose in Evolution*, p. 15. 1931.

30

canvases had a glory, a radiance, which dances through our hearts to this day.

That is how the stars were, to the simple men who followed beauty in the age of Faith. And that, it seems, is how the stars are to the wise men who follow reason in the age of Doubt. Does that not mean *something* to you? Does it not seem as though, after all, we may be able to surmount the first hurdle in our treasure hunt, the hurdle of the Universe?

I X

We have now reached the point where Shelley's assertion that 'it is impossible to believe that the spirit that pervades this infinite machine begat a son upon the body of a Jewish woman' looks rather less convincing than before. If our little earth is, as the scientists now assert, a solitary and awe-inspiring exception in the Universe, it looks as if it had been chosen, by that Spirit, for some particular revelation.

We may be wrong, of course. The scientists may be entirely misleading us. And one of the reasons why the average man may feel inclined to question Eddington, Fleming, Thomson, Jeans and the rest, is because it seems almost impossible to believe that so many millions of worlds should have been created for nothing.

'Such waste . . . such unparalleled profusion . . . such Titanic fecundity . . . how can it be? A limitless sea-shore for a single grain of sand? An endless roadway for a single speck of dust? I can't believe it.'

Have you ever held in your hand the seed pod of a common poppy? Shake it out. Thousands of tiny seeds, like sand, pour through your fingers. Enough to incarnadine the rolling fields, as far as the eye can see. Enough to bring oblivion to many men. Yet, if you scatter those seeds to the wind, only a few will take root. The fields will be no redder in the year to come than they are on this sunlit afternoon. Here and there a scarlet torch will burn in the long grass, but the rest of them, the bonfire, the conflagration that once you held in your fingers, what has happened to it? Who has blown it out? All we can say is that some seeds fell by the wayside, some fell upon stony places, some fell among thorns, but others fell on to good ground. It is the way of God.

This same phenomenon of apparent waste, of almost wilful prodigality, is evident to every man who has ever given Nature a thought. It is in the sky, in the breath of every wind, in the heart of every clod of earth. It seems to be the law of our own strange world. Why then should it not be the law of the universe?

Still the Immensity remains, you may say. All those noughts . . . they still worry me a little.

If you go on like that, I shall begin to lose patience with you. You can be too impressed by noughts. Have you never thought that if it is merely a question of numbers, you yourself, with your millions of red corpuscles in a single vein, can put up a brave showing against the most crowded channel of the stars? In you a million worlds revolve and as you walk down a simple country lane the doom of millions of tiny beings is written in every footstep. Do not talk to me of the Immensely great nor of the Immensely little. You are an example of both. And because you *know* that you are such an example you are outside the range of these petty measurements. Your soul is not an affair of the tape measure. It is so Immense that it shines beyond the coldest star. It is so small that it can only be seen under the Divine microscope.

x

We have now set our feet on the second rung of the hurdle.

On the first rung we observed, with the best possible authority, that this apparently insignificant little earth is unique in the universe.

On the second rung we observed that there is nothing in the laws of Nature, as we know it, to prevent us from believing that this little earth may be the only 'fertile' member of the immense galaxy of stars. To us it certainly seems an example of 'waste' on a Titanic scale, but this is merely one of many similar examples of the bewildering prodigality of Nature.

So far, so good.

But the third rung of the hurdle is rather more difficult. For on the third rung we have to ask ourselves why, even if these things are so, we have any right to assume that the guiding spirit of the universe is beneficent? (And in future it will really be simpler if we call that guiding spirit 'God'. The rationalist may call the spirit anything he likes, and so may the agnostic and the atheist. For us the spirit, the first cause, is God.)

By what conceivable reason can we call God 'good'? By what wild denial of the evidence of our senses can we assume that He is even in the least interested in us? Is not the evidence of Waste, which we have previously quoted in our favour, also capable of being quoted against us? Is He not capable of blasting the whole race from the face of the earth with His scornful breath, just as He has created whole tribes of animals, merely to destroy them?

And by the way, adds the rationalist, have we forgotten our little trouble over the cat and the mouse?

No, we have not forgotten it. And in a moment that little trouble, which has worried so many moralists since time began, will be brought forward as evidence for the defence. But first I want to ask you a question, not about God but about man. It is very important that you should answer it honestly.

Do you agree that man has a moral sense?

Do you agree that he has, on the whole, a general idea of what is Right and what is Wrong?

Let me meet some of the arguments which may make the rationalists answer this question in the negative.

The first and most obvious retort that the rationalist will make is that man is a moral animal only because and so far as he is a social animal.[1] In other words that Right and Wrong are merely matters of convenience, and that any sense he may have of these qualities spring only from his obligation to keep the laws of society.

I do not believe this to be true. I do not believe that

---

[1] See *The Belief in Personal Immortality*, by E. S. P. Haynes, the most brilliant and lucid statement of the Rationalist case yet published.

man's deep sense of right is only an outcome of society. That seems to me very like putting the cart before the horse.

But even if I did believe it, may I ask how it makes the smallest difference?

Who made society? Man. Why did he make it? For his own convenience and safety.

Then why, in the midst of this society (which we are asked to regard as purely utilitarian) do nearly all its members, in some way or other, at some time of their lives, perform acts of heroic unselfishness, acts which may even be *anti-social*, merely because they feel it Right to do so? It is no use telling me that they do it at the urge of a false religious teaching. The atheist is capable of acts of magnificent self-sacrifice as well as the Christian. It is no use telling me, either, that they do it through any reverence, conscious or unconscious, for Society. The lives of the anarchists knock *that* nail on the head. Nor is it any use telling me that this sense is the evidence of a sound training, or a good grounding in philosophy. An idea has to begin somewhere. Where did this idea begin?

Where did it begin?

And not only has the rationalist to answer that question, but he has to answer the equally hard question of what keeps it alive to-day? What is the explanation of this strange sense of Right and Wrong which is brooding over the whole world? You can no more deny it than you can deny the existence of the sun and the clouds. In fact, if I were feeling in a less conciliatory mood, I might be prepared to argue that the sense of Right and Wrong is implanted even in the animals. Certainly, in the most elemental matters of morals and marriage it is implanted in some animals a good deal more strongly than it is implanted in some of the inhabitants of Mayfair.

But after all, the best way to answer this question is to look into your own heart. At some time or another, you have been cruel. You have snubbed somebody, or hurt him without reason — you have, perhaps, laughed at his love, sent him away empty-handed. And when you had done that, after it was all over, you felt a beast. You felt a bitter feeling of remorse. You would give anything to undo what you had done.

Well — why did you have that feeling of remorse? Because you remembered some Biblical text? I doubt it. So it probably wasn't 'religion' that gave it to you. Because you had been told by your schoolmasters to be kind? Hardly. One doesn't usually either remember or wish to remember what most schoolmasters tell one. So it probably wasn't 'education' which gave it you. Because of some abstract feeling for your duties to 'society'? The question is so foolish that it need not be answered.

Where then did you get that feeling of remorse?

Is it not the simplest thing, the truest and by far the most sensible thing, to answer that you got it from God?

XI

If you still feel inclined, after this, to deny that man has a moral sense which is instinctive, and independent of society in any form, then I am afraid that you and I must part company, here and now.

You must step off the third rung of the hurdle, and re-
trace your steps. We shall say good-bye to you regret-
fully, because it looks very dark behind you, and it would
seem that you have nowhere to go, except to a vast and
singularly gloomy jungle. Still, if you feel that the jungle
is your spiritual home (which is what the rationalist is
constantly asserting, however violently he may deny it)
you had better get back to it as soon as possible. Meanwhile, our feet are beginning to be planted rather more
firmly on the third rung.

We will now suggest to you a very simple little proposition. It is so simple that some people may feel there
is a 'snag' in it. I felt that myself. However, in spite of
the most arduous self-examination, I do not see the snag.
The proposition is as follows:

(It will be remembered that we decided to describe the
spirit of the universe, the First Cause, by the simple, all-
embracing word 'God'.)

Man's nature was given to him by God.

Man has a moral sense.

If God has not a moral sense, God gave man something
which He did not possess Himself.

Which is absurd.

Therefore, God has a moral sense.

I was never any good at Euclid, but certain propositions
were so crystal clear that they penetrated even to my
grossly unscientific intelligence. The above little moral
proposition seems to me as clear as the first problem in
Euclid. Of course, if you deny the premises, the proposition is valueless. But if you are one of those who deny

the premises, you will by now have parted company with us and be hastening back to your jungle.

Let us now see where we have reached, in the hurdle race. To put it very briefly we have decided that we are the inhabitants of a planet, which, for reasons best known to God, is of unique and solitary importance. And we have decided that whatever God's intentions may be towards that planet, He must have, to say the least of it, as strong a sense of what is right and wrong, just and unjust, as the most intelligent men on that planet.

Our feet, then, are set very firmly on the third rung.

There is one more to be climbed. Perhaps the most difficult of all.

XII

On the fourth rung we have to decide, without any reference to any form of religion (for you will remember that we set out on the treasure hunt believing in nothing at all) whether there is any really definite evidence for the survival of the soul after death. It is obviously useless to discuss Christianity, or to attempt any sort of scientific investigation of the truth or falsehood of Christian history, if we begin with the idea that what we are going to prove is impossible.

Admit the possibility and then we can apply the microscope to the gospels to our heart's content. Deny the possibility and we might as well give up the whole pursuit.

It seems a vast problem to decide in one book, let alone in one chapter, particularly as we shall not attempt, at this stage, to avail ourselves of the evidence offered by the spiritualists. It seems even vaster when we decide that by 'survival of the soul after death' we mean, very definitely, the survival of *our* souls, *our* personalities, a resurrection of *ourselves*, and not merely a sort of 'gloomy merging' in the universe.

That phrase 'gloomy merging', by the way, is taken from the first act of Nöel Coward's delicate and diverting comedy, *Private Lives*. We will pause to examine it for a moment, because it is typical of the languid attitude which so large a number of Coward's generation, and mine, adopt towards the affairs of the spirit. It is, as far as I can recollect, the only occasion on which any of Mr. Coward's characters express an opinion about the next world. Their minds do not usually think much further ahead than the next party, which they are anxious to avoid if they have been asked, and anxious to attend if they have not.

However here, in an atmosphere of Molyneux 22, side-car cocktails and Schiaparelli pyjamas, and Cole-Porter gramophone records, the following dialogue suddenly flashes out:

ELYOT. Don't you believe in anything?

AMANDA. Oh yes, I believe in being kind to everyone, and giving money to old beggar women, and being as gay as possible.

ELYOT. What about after we're dead?

AMANDA. I think a rather gloomy merging into everything, don't you?

'A sort of gloomy merging into everything.' Yes.

And then, another cigarette, another side-car, and another Cole-Porter record, which I believe in those apocryphal days was called 'Night and Day'. We are back in this good old life again. And Death, whom Coward had brought before the footlights for a moment, even though he clothed him in the garments of a clown, makes a tactful and silent exit.

'Gloomy merging.' An admirable phrase. A much more pregnant phrase than we might at first suspect. For example, it happens to be a very good description of Buddhism, though I doubt if Amanda was acquainted with the doctrine of Nirvanah. It is also implicit in a good deal of the philosophy of the nineteenth century. Professor William James, in his famous *Varieties of Religious Experience*, constructs a hypothesis that 'the whole world of natural experience is nothing but a time-mask, shattering or refracting the one infinite thought which is the sole reality into those millions of streams of finite consciousness known to us as our private selves.' (Private *selves*, Mr. Coward, please!) And when finally a brain stops acting altogether, that special stream of consciousness which it subserved will vanish entirely from this natural world. But the sphere of being that supplied the consciousness would still be intact; and in that more real world with which, even while here, it was continuous, the consciousness might in ways unknown to us, continue still.

Well, if you can get any comfort from that, you are welcome. It seems to me only a highfalutin' paraphrase of Amanda's remark.

XIII

It would appear that Mr. Coward has led us slightly astray. Actually he has not done so; he has only given colour to the argument.

When we first considered him, you may remember, we were on the fourth and last rung of our preliminary hurdle, feeling slightly awed by the task we had set ourselves, which was the task of proving, without reference to any religion, the probability of human survival after death.

You will recall, again, that by human survival we meant a full and complete survival of our individual personalities – *not* merely a 'gloomy merging'.

Well, our discussion of 'gloomy merging' was not so irrelevant as it seemed, because the young person who made it is highly typical of the collection of people who parted company with us when the fourth rung of our hurdle was reached. They could not bring themselves to admit that man had an instinctive moral sense. And thus they were also precluded from admitting that it was possible to attribute any moral sense to the 'spirit of the universe', or whatever fancy name they like to give to God.

Strange as it may seem, we are going to call these people back for a moment in order that they may give evidence on our behalf. They may seem odd witnesses to call. Perhaps they are. And it is true that they can only give negative evidence. But negative evidence may sometimes have very positive results, as anybody who has ever had any experience of His Majesty's Chancery Court may agree. I believe that such may be the case on this occasion. It was only a moment ago that we parted from them, so they must be still within hailing distance. We call them — they come. It is good to see them again. We shall probably admit that we felt a little selfish when we allowed them to go off like that, into the night, into their spiritual jungle, while we pressed forward on our hunt for the treasure.

What we are now going to do, is to ask these people if they realize what their attitude, which at the highest may be called the doctrine of 'gloomy merging', implies. They probably don't. Very well — we will tell them. They will get the shock of their lives, because most rationalists, either through laziness or lack of courage, refuse to follow the implications of their convictions to the bitter end.

And since one of the essentials of good cross-examination is the element of surprise we will not waste another moment, but will tell them, without any polite preliminaries, one thing which they are asking *us* to believe.

We say to them:

'*You are telling us that the lives of Christ and of Nero are to be equally rewarded. You are putting Messalina and Joan of Arc in the same boat. You are asserting that Jack the Ripper and St. Francis of Assisi are, in death, one and the same. You are setting Michelangelo and Ivan the Terrible on the same pinnacle, or in the same dirty tomb. You are pinning medals, with equal diffidence, on the breasts of the cowardly and the brave, the cheater and the cheated, the ravisher and the ravished, the murderer and his victim. And*

42

it is really useless for you to mumble things about my working myself into a frenzy of rhetorical indignation, because I am not in the least ashamed of being indignant and my rhetoric could not possibly be dyed too deep a purple for the occasion. For you ... yes you ... are throwing all that is beautiful and all that is base on to a common dung-heap, and you try to evade the issue by talking airily about "gloomy mergings".'

Well, I don't happen to think that sort of thing is really so tremendously clever. I don't think the trick is worth the sacrifice.

Do you?

(By now the reader may have realized that I have unwittingly allowed myself to get into a state of what is sneeringly described as 'moral indignation'. I can't help that. It is not yet an offence against the laws of England to be either moral or indignant. And sometimes anger makes a man speak the truth.)

And I am angry with you, ———, or whatever your name is. Not so much because of your disbelief but because of your almost invariable refusal to face the consequences of your disbelief. If you said to me quite frankly that the whole world has straws in its hair, that the moon is a lunatic's eye and the patterns of the stars are like the scribblings of a silly child on a dark slate — a child who may put out its tongue in a moment of pique and wipe them away — if you said that to me, and then went out and shot yourself, I might have a little respect for you. But you don't. You shrug your shoulders and light another cigarette. And that is the sort of flippancy that I do not appreciate.

I know, as well as you do, the cruelties and injustices of this world, which cry aloud to God. And it is the very force of my own hatred of cruelty and injustice, which is *not* the result of education nor tradition, but is inborn, inbred, part of the very chemistry of my being — it is the force of this hatred which makes me realize that the somebody who gave it me must have it too. He could not have given the gift of pity to millions of men if he were not himself the fount of all pity.

Then why, you may ask, if he is omnipotent, does he allow pain? Why does he allow 'the cancer in the rose'? All I can say is 'I do not know'. Presumably I am not intended to know. I can only be thankful for the rose, and keep my faith that one day the meaning of the cancer will be clear to me.

XIV

And now, I fully admit we have been led astray. But I do not care very much, because at least our little outburst of indignation has cleared the air. It has enabled us to suggest to the people who refuse to accompany us on our treasure hunt that the jungle which lies behind them — (a jungle of their own creation) — is even darker and more infested with gloomy terrors than they had been inclined to imagine.

And having said that, I must instantly contradict the obvious retort, which will spring to some men's lips, that Faith, to those who have it, or think they have it, is only an inverted form of Fear. That they are so horrified at the thought of passing into darkness, or worse than darkness, that they will believe almost anything which offers them a sort of mental anaesthetic.

This retort, which is a very natural one, is usually called the Argument from Desire. The rationalists make a great deal of it. A great deal too much, in my opinion. For though, undoubtedly, there may be some whose faith is based on such treacherous foundations there are many others in whom the desire to believe has been, paradoxically enough, a positive deterrent from belief. Some of us have felt, so acutely, the shamefulness of believing because it was pleasant to believe, and shied, so instinctively, from a comforting creed because it *was* comforting, that a peculiar sort of complex was set up in us, which was the result, perhaps, of a super-honesty. There was something revolting, for example, in the idea of death-bed repentances – and, even now, I cannot rejoice in the story of the repentant thief on the cross, any more than I can really revel in the legend of the labourers in the vineyard. It is with the intellect rather than with the spirit that I savour these portions of the Christian tradition.

However, that is not the point. All I am diffidently suggesting is that the Rationalists are wrong to make so much about the Argument from Desire. It may be an important factor in the mentality of savage races. I do not pretend to know. It is not nearly so important a factor among educated persons as the rationalists would have us believe. In this day and age we have been 'had' so often, in the things of this world, that we are almost morbidly suspicious of being 'had' in the affairs of the next.

XV

I think we are very nearly ready to jump over the last rung of the hurdle. For our quarrel with the Rationalists suggested to us a very clear line of argument, namely that our own indisputable sense of justice probably comes from a universal fount of justice, and that if we realize that the inequalities of this world can only be redeemed in some future state, *He* must realize it even more clearly than we do.

Now you may remember that when we set out on this treasure hunt together we decided that we would begin by believing nothing at all. We had no faith, no creed, no knowledge, even, of any revealed religion. And if you will do me the honour of pausing, for one moment, to consider what has gone before, you will admit that the conclusions we have reached have been based simply and solely on the evidences of our senses, and not on any supernatural authority.

Very well. Supposing an ordinary, reasonably intelligent man had come out on this hunt with us and had reached the fourth rung of the hurdle. And supposing that this man, by some freak of education, had never heard of Christianity (it is a difficult supposition, but try to imagine it) and had no knowledge whatever of the very name of Christ. And supposing we then asked him how he felt about things, in his position on the fourth rung — how he felt, for example, about the possibility of the survival of the soul after death. Is it very unreasonable to suggest that his answer might run along the following lines?

'Well,' he might say, 'I seem to have got to my present position in this search for truth without doing any conspicuous violence to my own intellectual integrity. I don't think I've drawn too wide a bow at a venture. I don't think I've "cooked" the arguments unduly. And I do believe that I shall go on, somehow, that my personality will endure. But there's one thing I don't understand.'

'What's that?' we ask him.

'I should have thought that this God we've found ourselves forced to suppose (unless we're prepared to admit that we're living in a criminal lunatic asylum) would have given us some sign. Some — well, some sort of revelation. I shouldn't have thought he'd have left us guessing to this extent. After all, we've had to invent everything for ourselves, our own code of morals, our own theories of rewards and punishments, even our own doctrine of survival. Now, if only there had been some divine *example* ... I can't think quite what it could be, but something like a sign written in the sky, centuries ago, maybe only a few words, just for a few minutes, or a scroll of the divine law, hung for a single night among the stars so that all men could see, and read, and hand down to us what they had read. Or even a voice, speaking over the land and the sea. . . .'

And as he says that, we seem to hear, drifting down the centuries, a Voice that says: 'This is my beloved son, in whom I am well pleased'.

XVI

Now I do not believe that we have taken undue liberties in suggesting that this is the sort of thing which the ordinary, average man, who had never heard of Christianity, would be likely to say. Given his knowledge of the earth's position in the universe, as the scientists have described it for us, given his deductions from his own moral sense to that of the God he is compelled to suppose, I do not see how he could very well refrain from making this criticism.

He wanted 'a sign written in the sky, centuries ago, maybe only a few words, just for a few minutes, or a scroll of the divine law, hung for a single night among the stars'.

The men of Faith, the happy men, the men with a light in their eyes and a song in their hearts, tell us that God gave us far more than a sign in the sky or the flash of a glittering scroll. They tell us that He gave us a Life, and that with us He died. They tell us that He took upon Himself the world's pain and the world's despair, and dispelled it in a single sacrament of love.

That is what the men of Faith tell us.

In the name of all that you hold sacred — and you *do* hold something sacred, whatever your creed or your lack of it — isn't it worth while trying to find out whether the men of Faith are telling the truth? If there is only one chance in a thousand, isn't it worth it? Especially as we have seen (without any 'optimism' or 'faith', or even enthusiasm) that the Christian revelation is exactly the *sort*

48

of revelation which we, as members of the jury, would be likely to expect?

We need not discard our scientific apparatus. In fact, we clutch even more firmly to our microscope, our tape measure, our stethoscope and all the rest of it. We are not 'convinced'. No, not by a long chalk. But we do feel that there is, to say the least of it, enough evidence to give us just the right amount of impetus to leap over this hurdle that has so long been delaying us — the hurdle of the universe.

So — here goes.

But, what's this? What's happened?

We rub our eyes. We stare about us. We hold tight to our microscope, which seems the one sane thing in a very strange, wild world. And as we look behind us, we see, to our astonishment, that the hurdle has gone. Vanished utterly. What does this mean? Does it mean that we invented it? That it was all a dream?

We cannot tell. All that we know is that we are staring into a great darkness.

And then, we turn round. Slowly, not quite certain as to what we shall see. There seems to be a light somewhere. But we are not sure from where the light comes. It must be a very bright light, for we cannot look at it. We stare at the ground ahead of us.

And on the ground, we see a shadow. An immense shadow, thrown athwart the earth. We press forward — we are nearly in its embrace — when we halt. For we see that the shadow is shaped like a cross.

We close our eyes. We do not fall on our knees, nor pray, nor show any outward signs of emotion. Remember, we are gentlemen of disbelief. We are polite agnostics. Besides we have a tape measure in our pocket. It is to the tape measure that we are trusting, not to any crucifix, smouldering with ancient rubies and dimmed with the tears of centuries.

And so we take out our tape measure, and begin to take the measurements of the cross.

And only too late do we realize that somehow or other, by some queer fluke of chance, we have fallen on our knees.

CHAPTER II

HISTORY OR HYSTERIA?

I

A TAPE measure, and a crucifix.

In the one hand, a magnifying glass, in the other a Bible.

On the one side doubt, on the other Faith.

Can the two be reconciled? That is what we have to find out.

Remember, we are still agnostics. We don't really 'believe' in anything. But even the most sceptical of us may feel inclined to agree that there is a certain significance in the fact that as we studied, in the last chapter, the various designs of the universe, as we pondered the secret of the rhythm of space, and as we examined the pattern of our own spirits, we were forced to admit that somehow or other these designs, rhythms and patterns all had a common denominator in the symbol of the Cross.

Whether it was a lowest common denominator or a highest common denominator is yet to be seen. The fact remains that without any 'cooking' or figures, and without drawing any unreasonable deductions from the evidence, it did seem that it was easier to believe than to disbelieve the great primary fact that this little earth is of unique importance in the vastness of space, and that the spirit who directs it must have at least as clear an idea of justice as the men who inhabit it.

So our feet are on firm ground for the moment, and we feel that we can step forward. But no sooner do we start than we see that there is another big hurdle ahead of us. It is the old question of Immensity again, in a different form. Not space, nor the terrible prodigality of the stars, but Time. The fact that the hands of the eternal clock appear to stretch into infinity fills us with misgiving. Of what importance can be the nineteen hundred years after A.D. 1 compared with the apparent infinity of years that went before? We stare up at the hurdle with puzzled, discouraged eyes.

11

I remember being very depressed, as a small boy, by a diagram of Time which I discovered in a manual of popular science. It showed a long winding road, representing the history of the earth's inhabitants as they are known to man. The road had a 'time-length' of some 2,000,000,000 years. The first part of it was lost in fire and smoke. Then came a horde of very slimy-looking creatures, of the Lower Palaeozoic age, zoophytes, trilobites and the like. Further forward came a quantity of peculiar reptiles, Plesiosaurs, Ichthyosaurs and so on, all paddling along as if they were intent on getting jobs in 'King Kong'. It was only in the near foreground (if I rightly recollect, it was about 50,000 years ago, before the climax of the Fourth Glacial Age) that we came to a form of man at all, and even then it was only Neanderthal man whom we encountered. For Man as we know him (a very different creature) was born only yesterday. A mere matter of 30,000 years ago.

Now this picture greatly worried me, although to-day (if you will forgive a moment's irrelevancy) I must admit that these sort of statistics have rather lost the power to impress. Not because I doubt their accuracy — I am sure they are as accurate as anybody could desire — but because they all seem to bear the stamp of Mr. H. G. Wells. Whenever I open a popular magazine and find coloured plates of large, heavily-moustached creatures wallopping about in extinct coal-forests, I seem to see, in the long grass behind them, the plump, pink figure of Mr. H. G. Wells, disguised as a miniature Dinosaur, taking notes for future serial publication. It is doubtless impolite of me, but there it is. I have a profound conviction that the Neanderthal man was a little self-conscious, because he knew what an important part he was going to play in the *Outline of History*.

However, as a boy, I was depressed. For 2,000,000,000 years the earth had been the earth. If God made the earth, and is all-seeing and all-knowing, if the pages of the Future were to Him as an open book, then He must already have scanned, with a sublime sorrow, the lines of history which tell the dark story of the crucifixion. Must have stared over infinite horizons into the yet uncharted voyages of man. Why then did He spend such an extremely long time turning a reptile's scale into a bird's feather? Lengthening a bone here, shortening one there? Curving a spine, changing the colour of a skin, juggling with the subtle chemicals of a lizard's blood?

Time — it swept over me like a dark cloud. I was deafened, maddened by the ticking of the Eternal Clock.

III

Now, if you and I are to continue this journey together we had better admit that we are likely to encounter certain things which we do not understand. However bravely we may flourish our microscopes and however arrogantly we may extend our tape measures, we shall occasionally see nothing under the microscope and find that the thing we are measuring is like the rainbow. It is always over the hill.

Then is the whole hunt off? We set out to *prove* Faith, by rule of thumb. Must we now admit defeat, and throw away our tape measures?

I do not see why we should do that, even in face of the immensity of Time, provided that we keep our heads and do not allow ourselves to be dizzied by mere figures.

For what are the facts? Over an infinite number of years the world was being prepared for man. With an infinite intricacy of development life crept slowly from the edges of the sea to the dry land. From fish to reptile, from reptile to bird and mammal, and so to monkeys and sub-men. For this preparation God required not a million years but two thousand million years.

And then suddenly, as it were yesterday, the history of mankind begins. Nobody knows how the first man was born — and however closely we may study such remains as the Rhodesian skull which was discovered at Broken Hill in 1921, we are still without the 'missing link'. It may be 'unscientific' to suggest that there may be no such thing as the 'missing link' but if it is unscientific it is up to science to produce that link. The scientist tries to have it both ways. He says, with bland assurance, 'Man is certainly not divine because we have infallible proof to that effect in the missing "link".' It is as though a detective were to say, 'I am quite certain that X is a murderer because of the condition of Y's corpse, which, unfortunately, nobody has yet been able to discover'. If we define science as the 'classification of facts and the recognition of their sequence and relative significance', we are being just as 'scientific' as the scientists if we cease to stare into dark caves and turn to look up to the stars — if, instead of presupposing this perpetually missing link we say that the breath of God suddenly flickered over the world and man was born. For really, even after you have read *The Origin of Species* (a task which many of its most fervent admirers appear to have omitted) you are not very much wiser than when you read the first chapter of Genesis:

'*And God said, Let us make man in our image, after our likeness: and let them have dominion over the fish of the sea and over the fowl of the air and over the cattle and over all the earth and over every creeping thing that creepeth upon the earth.*

'*So God created man in his own image, in the image of God created he him; male and female created he them.*'

Now all this may seem to be very old fashioned, and may be it is. All I am trying to suggest is that it is foolish to be bothered by the vastness of Time when as far as we are concerned we only have to bother about thirty thousand years, which is a figure any child can imagine without difficulty. The vastness of Time need not concern man because for nearly all of Time as we know it the curtain had not yet risen on his little drama. What God was doing behind that curtain throughout infinity need not really concern us. The only thing of which we can be quite certain is that He was preparing scenes of incredible beauty — for somebody. And that somebody was man.

And when that curtain was raised, at last, the whole drama of history seems to lead swiftly, inevitably to the great climax of the Cross. Comparative historians will object strongly to this statement which is admittedly sweeping. They may point to the development of other religions in other countries, to high states of civilization (for example in Peru), which flourished only to die away. It would be altogether outside the scope of this essay to attempt to correlate those religions and civilizations. All I can suggest is that the Rationalist can have no really overwhelming reason for denying that the year A.D. I is at least not a wildly improbable year for a 'revelation'. God might have chosen the year 30,000 B.C., but He would not have had a very considerable audience to whom He could speak. He might have chosen the year A.D. 1936 too. However, we could go on till Doomsday like that. Let us therefore be generous, and admit that it all fits in.

'*If God were to reveal Himself to man, our tape measure tells us that the revelation might well have come when, according to the Christian, it did come.*'

IV

And so, you see, the chase is narrowing down.

We found that the limelight switched by the scientists focused itself on the earth.

By a deduction from our own minds we discovered it to be a kindly light.

By applying the tape measure we found that the brightest point of light might have been focused on the earth at approximately the time when Christians tell us that it was focused.

And so, we stuff our tape measures in our pocket, close our eyes, and jump.

Phew! We are safely over the hurdle of Time. We have landed on solid ground again. If we looked back we would see that it was not really nearly such a high hurdle as we had imagined. But we do not look back. For we see that the ground in front of us is strewn with documents. What are they? We step forward. We see that they are called 'gospels' and 'epistles' . . . 'acts' and 'revelations'.

With a quickening of the heart we start to pick them up and scan them. We realize that we have found our first concrete clues in the hunt for Faith.

v

Now, in the normal treasure hunt, clues are scarce. A scrap of paper here, a tiny piece of fabric there, a footprint half-smothered in the sand, a ghastly speck of blood. Yet, from these faded fragments, what enchanting pursuits have been created by the masters of fiction! How convincing, too, the ultimate attainment of their quarry!

As for the historians, they seem to be able to reconstruct a whole epoch from a broken vase. To hear the whispers that echoed round it as the wine was drunk, to hazard a battle in the curve of its stem, to guess at a nation's decadence in the lustre that has gathered, like history's frost, around the tarnished rim.

We might therefore quite reasonably suppose that in this treasure hunt — by far the greatest hunt of all — the clues at our disposal would be exceptionally sparse. With such an immense prize in view it would seem only right that there should be hardly anything to help us. If we found even a single torn scrap of papyrus, or the ghost of a legend, or a piece of doubtful pottery, we should be grateful.

However, the first thing we have to note is that the clues are not at all sparse. On the contrary they are voluminous and various, and they include a number of documents which are the most precious material of the historian, i.e. contemporary letters. And there is another thing which we have to note, forgotten by people who pin their faith exclusively to the written word, which is that the value of these documents is enormously enhanced by the fact that it is supported by a living legend.

Of course the whole thing may be a forgery. A lie on an immense scale. Heaps of wise men will tell you that it is. And indeed, as we study these documents, our first impression is that these wise men must be right.

'*For here before us, are a number of scraps of paper which tell us that God came down to earth in the shape of a man, Jesus Christ, who died for our salvation. These pieces of paper are as clear as a time-table. A time-table informs us that if we catch a certain train we shall arrive at a certain station. The documents tell us that if we obey certain rules we shall arrive at a place called heaven.*'

It seems too utterly idiotic, in this day and age, when Greta Garbo is playing round the corner, and a skyscraper is going up next door, and the wireless is moaning in the accents of Mr. Bing Crosby. It seems a far, far tune played on a lovely but illusory flute, somewhere on the shores of the world, in the days when the moon was a child's bubble rather than the synthetic pearl which it is to-day.

And yet, if those documents *were* genuine?

Phew! We take out our handkerchiefs and mop our brows.

VI

Now I am fully aware that my constant insistence on the importance of deciding whether these documents are genuine may cause bitter offence to a large number of people who have been brought up to regard every word of the Bible as sacred.

But their censure can hardly be directed against *us*, because we are not 'believers', we are only agnostics, whose principal concern is that we should keep an open mind.

However, even if we *were* believers, even if we had

come to the end of the treasure hunt for Faith, and had found the treasure, I still think that we should be justified in pausing to address a few words of polite remonstrance to the men of faith, with regard to their own attitude to these documents which they love so dearly.

To these men of faith we say: 'Whoever brought you up to regard every word of the Bible as sacred was extremely misguided. The Bible is the most varied book in the world. Some of its pages are dross, others are pure gold. To insist that every page has an equal value and that every page is authentic is to do harm to the whole great book.'

And having said this we would go on to point out that the ignorance of many devout Christians about their own New Testament is quite extraordinary. Let me ask them a few questions.

'Do you know that all the most eminent critics agree that whoever wrote the gospel according to St. Matthew, it was *not* St. Matthew? Do you know that St. Paul was the one person who most emphatically did *not* write the famous 'Epistle of Saint Paul to the Hebrews'? Do you know that it is generally agreed that the second epistle of Peter was probably written long after Peter was dead?

Do you know that the beautiful story of Christ and the woman taken in adultery forms no real part of the Gospel according to St. John? Do you know that it is absent from all the oldest MSS., and that it is even queried in many of the later ones, where it is admitted? Do you know that even the most devout and conservative critics are exceedingly disturbed as to the authenticity of the miracle (mentioned in Matthew only) of Peter casting a hook into the sea and bringing up a fish with a shekel in its mouth?

Have you ever heard of Q?[1] Are you aware that this is an hypothetical 'lost Gospel' which the scholars have been forced to assume in order to account for hundreds of striking similarities between Matthew and Luke, which are *not* in Mark?

Are you aware that although the story of our Lord's Virgin birth is a vital part of the Christian tradition, and although the gospel according to St. Mark is undoubtedly the oldest of the four gospels (much of Matthew and Luke being copied almost straight from Mark), yet the story of the birth is not in Mark at all? And if you were aware of it what is your answer to the very disquieting suggestions made by many eminent critics that the whole story is a pious fiction?

Are you aware of the storms which have raged round the Gospel according to St. John? Are you aware that even Dean Inge who can hardly be described as prejudiced in favour of the rationalists, admits that 'instead of preserving for us the words of Jesus Christ it contains merely free composition by the writer himself?' Have you ever pondered the significance of the fact that whereas the first three gospels describe Christ's ministry as extending over one, or possibly, two years, and as being carried out in Galilee, John makes it extend over three years, and tells us that it took place in Jerusalem? Have you ever wondered why such a stupendous miracle as the raising of Lazarus, which St. John recounts, should not receive even a passing reference in *any* of the other gospels?

[1] From the German *Quelle*, a source.

It is really vital that we should ask ourselves these and many other questions like them, and that we should find an honest answer to them. I have no desire to 'offend a simple faith', but, as I have stated before, I have no use for a faith which is not founded on fact.

That is why I am as eager as you are to start to work on these documents at once, with the microscope and the tape measure.

But first there is another class of critic whom we must answer. Not the devout believer in the sacredness of the Bible, but the man who says: 'Why all this fuss about the documents being genuine? What does it matter? You've got Christ's legend and teaching and example — everything that counts. Why bother about whether it's historical or not?'

The chief upholder of this point of view is Bernard Shaw. We will pause to address a few words to him.

VII

In his brilliant preface to *Androcles and the Lion* Shaw adopts towards the personality of Jesus exactly the same attitude as most men adopt towards the personality of Shakespeare, saying, 'We don't care whether Shakespeare was Shakespeare or whether he was Bacon or anybody else you like to mention. We've got the plays and that's all that matters.'

He writes:

'We have always known that Jesus had a real message, and have felt the fascination of his character and doctrine.

Not that we should nowadays dream of claiming any super-natural authority for him. But when, having entirely got rid of Salvationist Christianity, and even contracted a prejudice against Jesus on the score of his involuntary connection with it, we engage on a purely scientific study of economics, criminology and biology, and find that our practical conclusions are virtually those of Jesus, we are distinctly pleased.'

Shaw sums up his own fallacies, and tumbles headlong into a well of illusion in the following words:

'We must face the question whether, if and when the will-to-believe the miraculous side of the gospels fails us, there will be anything left of the mission of Jesus. Whether, in short, we may not throw the gospels into the waste-paper basket. I venture to reply that we shall be, on the contrary, in the position of the man in Bunyan's riddle, who found that the more he threw away, the more he had!'

Now it is most important that we expose this fallacy of Shaw's, once and for all, because it is a fallacy which he shares with millions of other loose-thinking persons. We are constantly meeting people who say, gaily, 'Of course, nobody believes in Hell nowadays' (in itself, a highly inaccurate observation), and we are constantly reading articles in the popular papers in which emphasis is laid on the 'beauty' of Christianity, or its 'practicability' or its 'modernity', while all the time the flaming fact of its *truth*, or the hideous fact of its falsehood, is calmly ignored.

Do the people who live in this Christian no-man's-

land, the people who think that Jesus was 'a most exceptional man, my dear, really *too* remarkable, greater than
Shakespeare even, or Beethoven . . .' do these people who
set Jesus on an earthly pedestal, forgetting that by their
action they are dragging him from the heavens, do they
realize the absolutely terrifying implication of their
attitude?

Mind you, I am not saying they are wrong. I am only
asking them if they realize what they are implying.

They are implying that for nearly two thousand years
the world has been in the thrall of a Jewish lunatic. They
are implying that the most exquisite creations of art, the
most sublime examples of heroism, the whole fabric of
decent government in the western world, has been
executed at the command of a crazy Oriental who could
no more rise from the dead than he could get out of a
strait-jacket and could no more feed five thousand than he
could buy a herring if he hadn't the cash on him.

These, gentle readers, are the alternatives. And I want
you to realize the sort of problem that this intellectual
honesty will force us to face.

It means, for example, that when we talk about the
resurrection we must not imply a merely 'spiritual'
resurrection, nor a mere survival of the dead man's ideas,
nor a pious legend derived from a hotch-potch of Greek
manuscripts. We must imply that on a certain hour
between night and day, in an Eastern tomb, there was a
strange stirring, while immense and incalculable forces
poured back life into the body of a dead man, so that he
was able to rise up and walk out into the moonlight. We
must imply this and nothing less. We must believe the

64

thing happened; it must be so real to us that we must be able to hear, in our hearts, the faint sigh in the tomb as the life-spirit flooded back into the tortured body, must be able to smell, in our own nostrils, the medley of strange scents which floated back to him, the scent of spices, and dust, and stale blood.

Can we persuade ourselves, beyond any shadow of doubt, that these things happened, merely by a cold-blooded examination of the evidence?

That is the tremendous question we have to ask ourselves. It is certainly the greatest question with which we shall ever be faced in this earthly life.

And now for the documents in which, somewhere, the answer is hidden.

VIII

Now I have not the faintest fear, in this volume, of making myself ridiculous, exposing my own ignorance and laying myself open to the most penetrating shafts of criticism, because it was perfectly obvious, at the beginning, that I should have to do so. No man who honestly tries to face all the facts of life and death can help tripping up, a great many times, to the infinite delectation of the crowd.

Therefore I do not mind confessing to you that until comparatively recently I was in a state of complete ignorance as to the originals of the documents on which the Christian faith was based. By 'originals' I mean the actual earliest manuscripts. Who wrote them? Where were they? Were there any contemporary manuscripts, i.e. had any man actually set down any words of Christ while Christ was still living? If so, who? And how?

We ought to ask ourselves these questions. I hold a Bible in my hands. It is printed on flimsy paper with gilt edges. Published at the University Press, Oxford. An utterly astonishing volume. The frontispiece tells me that it is

The
HOLY BIBLE
containing the
Old and New Testaments
Translated out of the Original Tongues and with the former Translations diligently compared and revised
by His Majesty's special command.

Over the page I find a long and somewhat fulsome address 'To the most High and Mighty Prince James, by the Grace of God, King of Great Britain, France and Ireland'.

King of France, etc.

And then, opening the book at random, I read the lovely words:

'*I am the vine, ye are the branches: He that abideth in me, and I in him, the same bringeth forth much fruit; for without me ye can do nothing.*'

One would say those words were enough. Yet who wrote them? How? When? With what ink on what paper? That is what I want to know. And as we are both engaged in the same vital search, let us try to answer that question.

The first thing we have to realize about these documents may come as a shock to us.

They are not contemporary.

In no part of the world, as far as we know, does there exist a scrap of manuscript, concerning Christ, which was written at the time of his life.

'The original autographs of the New Testament books have perished, and though some fragmentary pieces of an earlier date have been preserved, the oldest of our great MSS. are hardly older than about A.D. *350.'*

When I first realized this, a sort of chill crept over me. Those 350 years seemed to assume an immense importance. They were like a dark chasm which lay between me and the light.

Then, the briefest reflection showed the puerility of these sentiments. For one thing, there was the living legend of Christianity, which had never been broken, and in a moment I shall have something to say concerning the importance of that legend.

For another, there is the fact that this lack of contemporary manuscripts about the great classical figures of the past is the rule rather than the exception.

If we are going to deny the history of Christ merely on the grounds that we do not possess any absolutely contemporary documents, then we must also deny, on the same grounds, the existence of such men as Caesar and Cicero. Indeed, we should have a great deal more reason for denying the existence of these admittedly substantial persons, because there are no manuscripts of either Caesar or Cicero *within eight hundred years of their time.*

Now unless we are to spend a lifetime poring over codices, and puzzling ourselves with uncials and cursives, we had better trust to the experts, lay as well as ecclesiastical, that a large percentage of the books of the New Testament are genuine, i.e. that they are authentic copies of documents originally written within living memory of Jesus Christ, and that these original documents were written by the men who were supposed to write them, in good faith. Wherever there is any doubt the reader will have to take my word for it that I have inclined to the sceptical view rather than to the orthodox.

All the same, even if we find, after a good deal of research, that the majority of the documents are as trustworthy as any other historical documents, those documents are still a little unreal to us.

Or perhaps I should say they were unreal to *me*. I wanted to see the pen dipped in the ink, to visualize the first words of the New Testament as they were actually written. And little by little, I found that this was the picture which materialized.

Scene. A room in Jerusalem.

Time. A.D. 48.

Dramatis Personae. St. Paul, Timothy and Silvanus.

Paul is a short middle-aged man with weak, screwed-up eyes, and hands that are coarsened with the constant rubbing of the black hair-cloth which he used in his trade of tent-making. Timothy and Silvanus are young men. We do not know what they look like, but we know that Silvanus is probably the more intelligent, for there are certain signs that it was he who also wrote at the dictation of Peter.

Paul is dictating. Partly because that was the custom among busy people, partly because his weak eyes made it more than ever necessary.

He dictates with fire, using abrupt, staccato sentences, and all the time that he is dictating his hands are busy with the hair-cloth.

The sunlight streams in on to the papyrus. It is a roll of about three feet long, such as you could buy in any shop. It is about a foot wide. And slowly, surely, the papyrus is being covered with little columns, two or three inches wide.

Paul's voice rises and falls:

'Paul and Silvanus and Timothy unto the Church of the Thessalonians in God the Father and the Lord Jesus Christ. Grace to you and peace.'

With a nervous gesture he throws aside the hair-cloth and rises to his feet:

'*We give thanks to God always for you all, making mention of you in our prayers.*'

It would be improper to allow imagination to flicker any further over the pages of the scriptures. But this brief excursion may perhaps be forgiven. For those extracts which we have just quoted were from St. Paul's Epistle to the Thessalonians. The Epistles are the earliest documents of Christianity. This epistle is the first of them all. And the date of it is A.D. 48.

And so we have arrived, by means with which the most sceptical historian cannot quarrel, at a little man sitting

down in the sunlight, some fifteen years after that crucifixion which was to stab the heart of the world, and writing
the things which he believed, the things which were
dearer to him than life itself.

X

Now if you share my desire to 'see the works', this little
picture of the first man sitting down fifteen years after the
crucifixion to write the first words which we possess about
Christ may have made the New Testament rather more
real to you. But the very fact that it was a dated and
detailed picture makes us at once ask a very obvious
question:

'Why did they have to wait fifteen years before making
a record of these astonishing things? What had been
happening in the meantime?'

That question is easily answered. The earliest
Christians could not have seen the necessity for any written
record, for the very simple reason that they believed the
world was about to come to an end, and that at any
moment they would be transported to heaven to join
Christ in glory. This belief was still persistent even when
Paul wrote his letter to the Thessalonians, which we have
just quoted, for in it he says:

For the Lord himself shall descend from heaven with a
shout, and the dead in Christ shall rise first. Then *we
which are alive and remain shall be caught up together
with them in the clouds, to meet the Lord in the air*: and
so shall we ever be with the Lord.

It would seem, indeed, futile to men who cherished such a belief that they should sit down and write. There was not time. The pen might be struck from their hands by a thunderbolt.

It was only later, as one by one those who had been in close contact with Christ began to die away, that any need came to be felt of setting on record the things which they believed. In the meantime, they had the Epistles, which were passed round and copied by the various branches of the church, which was growing with astonishing rapidity.

Therefore we may say, as we study these documents in which, somewhere, the treasure is hid, that for the historian they are the right *sort* of documents, and they are the right *sort* of date. That may not be a very great advance, but at least it justifies us in continuing our study of these documents.

Now one of the troubles about this book is that it demands rather more than the usual co-operation between author and reader. However it is possible to make tha co-operation rather exciting, at any rate in this particular instance. For I am going to ask you to read the epistles with a particular object in view, the object of discovering the most extraordinary *omission* in all of them. Will you do this? And will you bear in mind the fact that you are looking, not for some piece of historical evidence which has been put in but for some piece of historical evidence which has been left out?

You won't? You are too busy? All right. Perhaps it doesn't matter very much. We can assume that I have read the epistles for you so that we share this discovery together. It is so simple that at first we may not apprehend it. But its simplicity must not blind us to its importance. *It is merely the fact that the authors of the epistles did not explain themselves.*

That, I am well aware, may seem to be an anti-climax. But it is not really an anti-climax if you consider its implications. For, Lord knows, the authors of the epistles had enough to explain! Among other things they had to explain that the world had been turned upside down. But they didn't bother to do so. They assumed that it was too obvious to talk about at all. 'We really can't waste our time on things like that, which we all know' — that seems to be their attitude.

Let us get this point quite clear, so that we may appreciate its immense significance. And in order to do so, let us shift on the clock to the present day and age, where we breathe more naturally, and make a comparison.

XI

Supposing a modern man wishes to convey to his friend that his business has never recovered from the shock of the war, what does he say? He says, 'My business has never recovered from the shock of the war'. In other words, he assumes that his friend knows what he means by the word 'war'. He does not think it necessary to say 'my business has never recovered from the shock of the war, which, Oh Titus, was waged between the British Empire, France, Italy, America, etc. against Germany, and in which, etc. etc.' He takes it for granted that the war was a fact so obvious that it needs no explanation.

Now this is precisely the attitude adopted by the authors of the epistles. The resurrection of Christ is regarded by them as something which is as indisputable, historically, as the death of President Wilson. It does not even occur to them to argue about it, any more than it occurs to an American senator, in a speech, to say 'since the death of President Wilson . . . that is to say, if he really is dead, and if his body was not mysteriously spirited away, and if he is not, at the moment, living in a hut in Georgia, covered with whiskers'. Such a senator would be rightly regarded as pedantic. The authors of the epistles would have regarded it as equally pedantic to write 'Since the resurrection of our Lord Jesus Christ, if indeed, he did rise again, and if the astonishing stories we believe are not untrue'.

'Astonishing', is indeed, a mild word for the things which these men believe. And 'believe' is a mild word for the intensity of their conviction. It is as though they said 'we know', rather than 'we believe'. And what do they know? They know something so stupendously difficult, so utterly against the common run of things, that you would imagine that nobody but a congenital idiot could give it even a moment's consideration, *unless there were overwhelming evidence in its favour*.

If I suddenly announced to the world that I had a cat which played the fiddle better than Kreisler, standing on its head, this would be a calm and boring platitude compared to the things which the authors of the epistles accepted as unquestionable *facts*.

And the authors of the epistles were not congenital idiots. Nor were they bemused by the kindly haze of distance, which lends enchantment to any view, particularly to the view of Messiahs. The authors of the epistles were within hailing distance, historically, of Christ, at any rate, when their ideas, which they afterwards transmitted to paper, were formed. The winds had hardly had time to efface the sacred print of his steps in the sands over which he walked. The rain had hardly had time to wash away, with its callous tears, the blood from the rotting wood of the deserted cross.

Yet, these men knew — I can't go on using the word 'believe', which is far too vapid and colourless — that God had descended to earth in the shape of a certain man, that this man had met an obscene and clownish death, and that the grotesque mode of his dying had redeemed mankind from sin. They knew, moreover, that he had risen from the dead on the third day and ascended into heaven. It is no use saying that their minds were prepared for such legends because of the prophets, and because of the immemorial Jewish tradition that this sort of thing would happen, one day. Our minds might be prepared for all sorts of things which, if they happened, would be rejected for their sheer improbability. But these men's minds did not reject these things. They accepted them implicitly. And at the risk of being a bore, I must reiterate the fact that they accepted something far more astonishing than a statement that the moon was made of cheese, or that little girls are made of 'sugar and spice and all things nice'. They accepted something infinitely more miraculous than that. They accepted the Christian tradition.

Now let us sum up our progress to date, as far as the documents are concerned, remembering that we have only considered the epistles.[1]

What do these show us? They show us a phenomenon which, at least, we cannot ignore — the phenomenon of men, who certainly cannot be described as simpletons, writing letters to members of a rapidly growing congregation, all of whom believed that something had happened in the world which was entirely unique and utterly incomprehensible, and believed it to such an extent that they didn't even trouble to argue about it.

You may say the thing didn't happen.

You may say the men were mad.

You may invent a thousand theories about dreams, visions, plots, conspiracies and the like.

The one thing you can *not* say is that the people on the spot did not hold this belief.

What belief, you may ask?

The belief that Christ had risen from the dead.

And that brings us inevitably to the gospels, and to our first miracle.

XII

It may seem a little early in the scheme of this book to apply the microscope and the tape measure to the tomb of Christ. It may be felt that we ought to see if we can jump over the hurdle of some quite little miracle first, and leave

---

[1] These conclusions are based entirely on the fourteen epistles which are recognized as genuine by all schools of thought, lay as well as ecclesiastical. No advantage has been taken of the seven 'suspect' epistles.

the great hurdles till the last, till a time when we have perhaps got into better spiritual training. But that would be not only cowardly but unhistorical.

It is better to examine the Resurrection, quite honestly now, and see if we can at any rate admit its possibility, from the documentary evidence, for the very simple reason that the Resurrection is the rock on which the church is built. Even if all the rest of the miracles were true, even if the whole life of Christ were exactly as the gospels narrate, nevertheless, if the story had ended in the tomb, there would have been no Church and no Christianity.

We have, in this case, to put all our eggs in one basket. St. Paul faced up to this grim alternative with startling honesty. He said:

'If Christ hath not been raised, your faith is vain; ye are yet in your sins. If *in this life only* we have hoped in Christ, we are of all men most pitiable.'

Now you will remember that we are still standing, with quite open mind, facing the documents which are spread out before us. There are so many documents that it all seems a little bewildering and I must ask you to trust me that we shall examine only those documents which have been approved as genuine by history.

The first document we pick up is called 'The Acts of the Apostles'. The Acts were written by St. Luke, who was a doctor, and they bear many marks of being contemporary. And we have not read more than a few verses of the Acts before we realize that we are face to face with a very singular situation. A situation which, as far as we know, has never had any parallel in history, before or since. For what do the Acts show us?

'They show us a company of men and women full of confidence, enthusiasm, and courage, ready to face persecution and death, eager missionaries. What has given them this new character? Not long before some of them had fled in dismay at the first threat of personal danger. When Jesus was crucified they had lost the last glimmer of hope that he might prove to be the Christ. When he was placed in the tomb, Christianity was dead and buried too. Now we meet these men and women a few weeks later and they are utterly changed. It is not that there is some faint return of hope among a few of them. All are completely certain that Jesus is indeed the Christ. What has happened to cause this transformation? Their answer is unanimous: on the third day he rose from the dead.'[1]

Now I have put this argument first because the certainty of Christ's resurrection by the early Christians is a matter of *history*. It is a historical *fact*, without any supernatural flavour about it at all. There was nothing supernatural about their hardships, their tortures, nor also about their radiant joy. You can say their belief was crazy, but you cannot deny the belief itself, nor can you deny that the belief was so entirely overwhelming that it made them sacrifice everything in the world for it, because those sacrifices are matters of history. We may be, of course, in a better position to put forward theories as to what happened in the tomb on Easter morning. But we must not forget that what we *think* is a good *theory* is

[1] *The Valley and Beyond*, Anthony C. Deane, p. 72 (Hodder & Stoughton).

completely different from what they were *certain* was a tremendous *fact*.

We are gentlemen of disbelief. But we are not gentlemen of such stubborn disbelief that we are going to deny the facts of history as well as the facts of religion. And the astonishing transformation of the early Christians is a fact of *history*.

What caused that transformation? It is up to the Rationalist to supply an answer. He will have to produce a pretty big answer. Let us look at some of the answers he supplies.

XIII

The first and most obvious explanation is that the disciples may themselves have stolen the body. That is the sort of thing we should expect the doubters to say to-day, and it is highly significant that it was exactly what the doubters did say at the time. For we have it on the authority of St. Matthew that the chief priests 'gave large money unto the soldiers saying, Say ye, His disciples came by night and stole him away while we slept. And if this comes to the governor's ears we will persuade him and secure you. So they took the money and did as they were taught. And this saying is commonly reported among the Jews until this day'.

Well, of course, St. Matthew may be a liar. The Jews may not have bribed the soldiers. The soldiers may actually have fallen asleep. The disciples may actually have stolen the body, you can believe anything you like.

But if you believe this, are you not believing something which is almost as difficult to believe as the Resurrection itself? It was not the habit of Roman soldiers, at any rate in the first century, to fall asleep so extremely soundly that they would be undisturbed by the rolling away of a large stone and the removal of a body. Moreover if they *had* fallen asleep, in this very unexpected manner, they would hardly be in a position to say whether the stone had been rolled away by the disciples or by some supernatural agency. And again, they were already liable to death, for these mysterious soldiers — and what would not the world give for their evidence! — had disappeared, leaving the tomb open and the body gone.

But really these arguments, though apposite, are mere pebbles compared with the immense historical rock of fact that the disciples *believed* the Resurrection, and were prepared to face humiliation, death in defence of their belief. If they themselves had achieved a 'fake' resurrection, to score off their opponents, and if they had concealed the body of Christ in some dark cellar of Jerusalem, how do you account for their subsequent behaviour? Men do not give up everything in life for a forgery, especially if it is a forgery which they have themselves committed. The subsequent behaviour of the disciples, which is not a matter of conjecture but of history, must seem to any reasonable man a complete and final answer to the suggestion that the body of Christ was *stolen* by the disciples themselves.

XIV

We are still asking the Rationalist to give us some explanation. As gentlemen of disbelief we will accept almost anything provided that it sounds reasonable. But it must account, somehow, for the transformation of the apostles, which is also history.

Where did the body go?

The Rationalist scratches his head and reverts to the theft theory. No — it probably wasn't the disciples. So it must have been the Jews.

The Jews? My dear Rationalist, you can't say that sort of thing, you can't really. It betrays such a lamentable ignorance of history. If the Jews *had* removed the body, the first thing they would have done would have been to exhibit it as publicly as possible in order to disprove the alarming tales which the hated Christians were spreading. Christ had been a bitter thorn in their flesh — so bitter that the Sadducees and the Pharisees had actually formed a coalition which eventually spelt his doom. Is it conceivable that these people, if they had been in possession of the one infallible proof which would have answered the Christian challenge, namely the body of Christ, would not have produced that body, have lain the lifeless corpse on the city's highest wall?

The same answer may be given to those who tell us that the Roman government had stolen the body. It seems difficult to believe that adult persons should credit such suggestions. The Roman government was interested in one thing and one only, the keeping of law and order. To show how ridiculous this theory is let us consider a very simple parallel. Supposing that a particularly troublesome sect of Indians elevated Mr. Gandhi, during his lifetime, to the position of a god, and prophesied that he would die in prison and that his body would then ascend to heaven. Supposing that Mr. Gandhi did die in prison. Is it even vaguely likely that the British government would steal the body of Mr. Gandhi and conceal it, knowing that by doing so they were deliberately inflaming the faith of the fanatics who believed the body to have ascended?

Where did the body go?

We don't seem to be getting very far with the theft theory. Let us see if we can approach it from some other angle.

XV

We don't believe in the Resurrection. It is impossible. I can't rise from the dead, you can't rise from the dead, and so nobody can rise from the dead.

Is that more or less what we feel about it? Perhaps it is. It was all very well for the Apostles. They expected something like that to happen. And when a man expects anything to happen . . .

But just a minute. We're going too fast. The disciples did *not* expect it to happen. The Resurrection was a *shock*. It came as a completely unexpected and bewildering occurrence which practically knocked them off their feet.

It is all very well to say 'Christ had foretold his own resurrection and the disciples ought to have been on the look out for it'. Maybe they ought to have been. But we are not concerned with what they ought to have felt but with what they did feel. And what they did feel is very clearly expressed for us in the twenty-fourth chapter of Luke. When Mary Magdalene and Joanna and Mary the mother of James and other women came breathless from the empty tomb, shaking with an extraordinary excitement, and stammering out the news to the apostles, we are told

'And their words seemed to them as idle tales, and they believed them not.'

Over and over again this point is emphasized. Every single one of the gospels insists upon it, with a variety of detail which bears a strange conviction. Read the story of Doubting Thomas, as it is narrated by St. John. Thomas said 'Except I shall see in his hands the print of nails and put my finger into the print of the nails and thrust my hand into his side, I will not believe'.

Eight days passed by. The disciples were gathered together. The doors were shut. And suddenly Jesus was with them. He cries out 'Peace be unto you'.

'Then saith he to Thomas, Reach hither thy finger and behold my hands; and reach hither thy hand and thrust it into my side. And Thomas answered and said unto him, My Lord and my God.'

XVI

'That is all very well,' says the Rationalist, 'but anybody can invent that sort of story.'

'Could *you?*'

'Well ... perhaps I couldn't. But any good novelist.'

'But when a novelist invents something he does it for
a good purpose, doesn't he?'

'What do you mean?'

'Well, he does it in order that he may sell his books
and make money. He doesn't do it in order that he may
be ... well, crucified upside down, like Saint Peter.'

'I don't know what you're getting at,' says the
Rationalist.

'All I'm trying to get at is a motive. We're both dis-
believers, aren't we? We're both on the same trail, aren't
we? Well ... where's the motive? All good stories have
to have a motive.'

'Yes,' echoes the Rationalist. 'All good stories. The
Resurrection's a damned good story. A magnificent piece
of fiction. And that's about all.'

And here I ask the Rationalist a few questions. But
first, let us sum up our progress very briefly, as gentlemen of disbelief. We must admit that it isn't very great.
We're faced with the *fact* that the body's gone. We don't
know where. We're faced with the *fact* that a large number
of men and women are utterly transformed. We don't
know why. We're faced with the *theory* that they were
all liars on a colossal scale. And, once more, we don't
know why, because their lies were driving the nails into
their own coffins.

Still, we are not too dismayed. Somebody invented it
all. That is what we say to ourselves. But here, once
again, we are up against a 'snag'. For, being honest, we
have to ask ourselves this question, 'What would a
novelist have done if he had been inventing the story?'

83

At the very least he would have given a description of how it all happened. He could not have resisted the temptation to describe the rolling back of the stone. He could not have failed to search his brain for the most glowing metaphors he could find in order to suggest the tremendous moment when a pale figure with bleeding hands appeared in the doorway of the tomb, paused, and glided into the night.

But the gospels are silent on this point.

And a novelist (for the Rationalists are implicitly accusing the disciples of being exceptionally brilliant novelists) would then have staged some very sensational 'come-back'. An apparition before the High Priest. A vision over Jerusalem. Anything you like.

But the gospels tell us nothing of such an apparition. Instead they tell us that he first appeared to Mary Magdalene. And moreover they tell us that when he did appear, he was not recognized.

XVII

And now I want to pause for a moment, and be rather personal.

The evidence I am going to suggest may not be of much value to you, but it is of value to me. And as I say, I have to be extremely personal about it, because that is the sort of evidence it is.

I am a fairly versatile man of letters. I have been almost every sort of journalist from a crime reporter to a dramatic critic, from a gossip writer to an editor of a magazine. I have published novels, essays, autobiographies, pamphlets, produced plays, revues, etc. etc. All these things may be, and probably are, ephemeral and without merit. That is not the point. The point is that it is hardly possible for a man who has had so much traffic with the written and the spoken word to avoid attaining a certain competence in judging the true word from the false.

Let me make this point clearer by an analogy. Certain learned judges, who over a period of many years have listened to the cross-examination of witnesses, acquire, after a time, a sort of sixth sense. 'That woman is lying', they say to themselves, and often, I have no doubt, they would find it difficult to explain exactly why they knew she was lying — they would only know that their mind was full of the echoes of past crimes and ancient falsehoods and half-forgotten treacheries, and that this woman's voice rang down that same dark gallery of liars.

Now this sixth sense is also bestowed, I believe, on those whose business it has been, over any considerable period, to sift the true from the false in literature. Consider the journalist. Any decent journalist — and there are lots of them drinking far too many double whiskies over the bars of Fleet Street — will be able to tell you, with absolute authority, when a story is faked and when it isn't. The general public may be deceived. They may think that Mr. X's weekly article on Mothers is too touching, whereas the journalist may know that Mr. X writes his article with his left hand and beats his mother with his right. The general public may think Lord Y's stirring call to England's youth really comes from the heart, whereas the little man in Fleet Street knows that as soon as Lord Y had written it he rang up his broker, sold a block of War Loan, bought Japanese industrials with the proceeds, and then went off to stay with a German blonde in the South of France. You can't fool Fleet Street. Sometimes I wish you could.

And I speak as a hard-bitten man of Fleet Street when I say that some of the Resurrection stories have an apparently unmistakable ring of truth. I say 'apparently' unmistakable because we can all tell stories of men and women who have uttered black lies to us while the light of truth and friendship shone on their faces. But no liar I have ever met in this world or ever hope to meet in the next was as good a liar as St. John when he told the story of how Christ appeared to Mary Magdalene.

You remember how it happened? She had visited the tomb. They had said to her, 'Woman, why weepest thou?'

'*She saith unto them, Because they have taken away my Lord, and I know not where they have laid him. And when she had thus said, she turned herself back, and saw Jesus standing, and knew not that it was Jesus. Jesus saith unto her, Woman why weepest thou? Whom seekest thou? She, supposing him to be the gardener, saith unto him, Sir, if thou have borne him hence, tell me where thou hast laid him, and I will take him away. Jesus saith unto her, Mary. She turned herself, and saith unto him, Rabboni; which is to say, Master.*'

Those two words.

The gentle 'Mary', echoing in the garden.

The breathless 'Master', as she saw his face.

If we believe that story, it is one of the loveliest things that the printed word will ever give us. It is a story over which, without shame, a man may weep.

If we do not believe it, it is a brilliant but shameful lie. Does it sound like that to you?

Does it sound a fake?

'*Jesus saith unto her, Mary. She turned herself, and saith unto him, Rabboni, which is to say, Master.*'

XVIII

'You are becoming emotional,' says the Rationalist.

'I should hardly be human if I weren't.'

'Possibly. But you are quoting exclusively for your own purposes. What about the discrepancies in the various accounts?'

'Show me some.'

The Rationalist, if he is like most of his kind, will probably turn, at once, to what is supposed to be the conflicting testimony of Luke and John, with regard to the appearance of Christ on Easter day. This is what Luke says:

'*And as they thus spake, Jesus himself stood in the midst of them, and saith unto them, Peace be unto you. But they were terrified and affrighted, and supposed they had seen a spirit. And he said unto them, Why are you troubled? and why do thoughts arise in your hearts? Behold my hand and my feet, that it is I myself: handle me and see.*'

Side by side with Luke's story he sets John's account of the same event. John says:

'Then the same day at evening, when the doors were shut where the disciples were assembled for fear of the Jews came Jesus and stood in the midst and saith unto them, Peace be unto you. And when he had so said, he shewed them his hands and his side. Then were the disciples glad, when they saw the Lord.

'You see?' says the Rationalist. 'One man says they are terrified and the other says they are glad. They can't both be right.'

On the contrary. I should strongly suggest that this discrepancy is exactly what makes us feel that they *are* both right. Terror at the sight of the unknown, joy at the amazing discovery that the shade is no shade but the Man they had loved — fear and ecstasy — horror and exultation — what else could we expect?

However, we will allow the Rationalist his little victory here, because he has such an enormous amount of other difficulties to meet. He has to account, in all, for twelve appearances. According to the witnesses (who, we must constantly remind ourselves, were bearing witness against their own interests) he appeared in Jerusalem, in Galilee, near Damascus, in a room, on a lake, on a mountain, on the road, to one at a time, to two at a time, to seven at a time, to five hundred at a time, walking, talking, sitting, standing, eating, drinking.

Let us consider this one instance — the appearance to the five hundred.

There is an old saying that forty thousand Frenchmen

can't be wrong. A brief study of the history of Europe since the treaty of Versailles is enough to convince one that forty million Frenchmen can be extremely and protractedly wrong. And so I suppose that five hundred Jews can be wrong too. But there is this difference between the Frenchmen and the Jews, the Frenchmen were dealing with natural events — if you can call the war a natural event — whereas the Jews were dealing with events so extremely extraordinary that the word supernatural seems a mild description of it.

Let me put it like this. If one man says he has seen a ghost you may believe him or disbelieve him according to your own view of the probability of ghosts and your own opinion of the veracity of the man in question. But if ten men tell you they have seen a ghost, at the same time and in the same place, you begin to sit up and take notice. And if five hundred men tell you they have seen a ghost — well, you must admit that you are in a somewhat startling minority.

And yet, we force ourselves into this minority if we deny the evidence of St. Paul's first letter to the Corinthians. *This letter, after being subjected to the fiercest scrutiny of the centuries, has stood up to every historical test.* In it St. Paul says:

'He appeared to about five hundred brethren at once, of whom the greater part remain until now, but some are fallen asleep.'

Now St. Paul was writing to *opponents*, who might easily have contradicted him. And St. Paul was a highly educated man. You may call him a lunatic, if you will, but you must admit that he was the sort of lunatic who, in 1936, would get a first at Balliol. And such lunatics, being endowed with cunning, do not make statements of this sort when at least three hundred people could instantly rise up and shout 'Liar!'

So in what position are we if we deny this story? We are in a position where we have also to deny the testimony (admittedly it is negative testimony) of at least three hundred persons who, at the date in question, thought they saw something which, we affirm, they could not possibly have seen. And the only reason we have for taking up this position is our fixed dogma that miracles, as Matthew Arnold said, 'don't happen'. And if you object to the word dogma, as applied to your convictions, I would suggest that you looked it up in a dictionary.

XIX

Now we have tried, perhaps not very successfully, throughout this long and detailed examination, to retain the agnostic pose, to keep our microscopes well polished and our tape measures from trembling. As far as our treatment of the *facts* of these documents of the Resurrection is concerned we have, I believe, taken no liberties to which the Rationalist could object. We have invented nothing and we have concealed nothing.

But gradually — as though we were archaeologists groping through the darkness of some corridor towards a tomb that for many centuries has lain hidden under the sand, we have discerned, through these documents, the glimmering of a pattern. A touch of gold here, a sparkle there, the glitter of a diadem, the radiance of a casual jewel, thrown into a corner. It is all muddled, it is true, it is all a chaos. But it is a glorious chaos, the sort of luxuriant tumble of beauty that glimmered, in the half-light, to the men who first thrust forward into Tutankhamen's tomb.

And as we look back over the evidence, sorting it out, scrutinizing it more and more eagerly, it seems as though a great many extraordinary things were suddenly happening. As though the microscope in our hands was turned into a diamond. As though the tape measure glittered with a strange gold. As though all the tangles and discrepancies suddenly straightened themselves out into a solitary and tremendous truth. As though the critics and the carpers had taken to their heels and vanished in a cloud of dust. And as the dust clears away, slowly, in the quiet Eastern twilight, we see a stone, and it moves — it moves.

X X

Is it all a trick? Are we all deluded fools, clinging with bleeding fists to a symbol just because it is a symbol? Are we conjuring up visions for ourselves because life, without the vision, is insupportable? Are we children of Nothing, trying to be children of Something?

Is the risen Christ a waxwork? Jerking its hands down the centuries in comfort to the craven and the fool?

And one of us might cry out, 'Am I hypnotizing

myself? Forcing my knees to bend in prayer? Posing?
Assuming an attitude? Closing my eyes because I dare
not open them? Oh God — that I might know the truth.
That I might throw away these petty measuring tapes
and magnifying glasses, which are but feeble flames with
which to lighten the infinite darkness! That I might be
pierced with faith, as a spear pierces, and glory in the
agony of certainty, rather than rot in the desert of doubt.'

X X I

We pull ourselves together. We feel a little shattered
by all this. We have been through a considerable
emotional experience which was all the more disturbing
because it was completely unexpected. We would not
have believed that an impartial study of a lot of dusty
documents could have quite such an effect on a man.

However, we feel better now. The sun is shining. We
are still in this world. The table is firm beneath our pen
and the floor beneath our feet. And though we are forced
to admit that the Resurrection of Jesus Christ is not only
probable, but is considerably more 'historical' than most
history, it is still comfortably vague to us. It has not yet
knocked us off our feet. We need a good deal more than
that before we can make up our minds.

And so we march on, gentlemen of disbelief, with
hearts that hope, and are yet afraid.

CHAPTER III

THE CROSS AND THE CRITICS

I

THE man next to me leant forward rather unsteadily, clutched the stem of his cocktail glass, leered at me with glazed eyes and said, 'But how do you explain St. John, eh? How do you get over *that* little difficulty?' He turned triumphantly to the barman. 'Saint John!' he blurted again, and winked heavily. But the barman's knowledge of English was very limited, and he apparently thought that Saint John was a new sort of cocktail, for all he did was to fill my friend's glass.

This sudden departure to the cocktail bar is neither irrelevant nor irreverent. For you and I are writing this book together, as it were, and if you feel as I do, you were probably rather embarrassed by the emotional outburst which concluded the last chapter. True, we had good cause for excitement. We had come quite a long way in our treasure hunt. By a process of cold reasoning we had concluded that we were of unique importance in this immense universe, that the spirit who ruled that universe was kindly disposed to us, and that if this spirit had desired to reveal His purposes to us He might well have done so round about A.D. I. That had brought us to Christ. Then, in the same spirit of cold reasoning we had 'tackled' the most difficult of all the Christian hurdles, the Resurrection, and to our great astonishment we found clue after clue which pointed to its truth, and all our efforts to regard it as a pious fraud led us into a morass of difficulties. With growing excitement we realized that this thing which we had regarded as a painted legend, a lovely romance, was standing up to all the tests of history. However much we tried to scrape away the paint, it still shone, true gold, and however much we tried to destroy the romance, it obstinately grew clearer and more luminous, until suddenly we were dazzled, and a little afraid.

And so, as gentlemen of disbelief, instead of going to some ancient church, and kneeling down and seeking enlightenment, we decided to come to the headquarters of polite paganism. Milton has no use for 'a fugitive and cloistered virtue, unexercised and unbreathed, that never sallies out and sees her adversary, but slinks out of the race, where that immortal garland is to be run for not without dust and heat'.[1] Neither have we. It would have been easy enough, after that first glimpse of light, to write the rest of this book in the cloister of some old church. But though it might have been a prettier book, and though its pages might have been stained with the blues and the greens of those windows through which generations of pious men have looked up to God, though its prose might have caught the rhythm of anthems and been fragrant with the breath of incense, it would have lost touch with the modern world.

For if St. John means less to you in a cocktail bar than in Westminster Abbey, then there is something wrong.

---

[1] Milton, *The Areopagitica*.

11

And so, we arrive at the Riviera. The car is stacked with books, Christian, Pagan, Spiritualistic, Atheistic, all clamouring to be read. They look somewhat out of place in the very modern sitting-room of the hotel. The only book, strange to say, which seems completely at home is the Bible, for it is square and shiny and black. It lies on top of a 1935 chromium-plated table, and the minute it was put there it seemed to become an integral part of the design. It was a fluke of course, but it was a curious fluke. If the man who had decorated this room had designed a book specially to 'go' with steel furniture, square sofas and metallic curtains, that Bible would have been the sort of book he would have chosen.

But the fluke was even more curious than that. For if he had also designed the contents of the book, searching for some legend or some tale which should be eternally appropriate to this little gilded fringe of coast, some proverb which could be read with profit by every man who might chance to lay his head in this room, he could have found no more superbly apposite words than those at which my Bible is now opened.

'And I find more bitter than death the woman whose heart is snares and nets, and her hands as bands; whoso pleaseth God shall escape from her, but the sinner shall be taken by her.[1]

Nothing that any of the most thoroughly hard-

[1] Ecclesiastes, vii, 26.

95

boiled American novelists could possibly say about
women could have a sting so acid as the prophet's words.

The women whose hearts are snares and nets — you
may see them in the hall every time you pass through,
looking very exquisite with their bronzed arms and their
drill skirts and their painted toes, leading a Borzoi by
one chain and a man by another. And yet, curiously
enough, you don't resent them as you used to do. Something curious has happened. For these women, lying on
the beach, oiling their naked backs and then lying face
downwards in the sand, prostrating themselves for hours
in worship of the sun — they do not seem to exist. The
corps of athletes, jumping over ropes, throwing footballs
at each other, splashing in the water, they all seem as
unsubstantial as a flight of midges at twilight. As for
the palaces, the luxury hotels and the villas, they are as
cardboard.

You don't get any 'evangelist' feeling about it. You
don't feel, thank God, that these women are 'wicked', or
even 'boring'. You do not feel you want to take the oil off
their backs nor the red off their lips. Nor do you feel that
an earthquake ought to come and wipe away these
glittering hotels. They are quite hideous, of course, but
they are comfortable and they are making money for
somebody. All you feel is, once again, that they aren't
solid. They are a strange painted mirage. And the only
thing that *is* extremely solid is the little book that lies
by your bed, the Bible.

It is difficult to explain this without appearing to be
'affected'. It is, indeed, difficult to explain, in any case,
because it is such a very odd feeling. But wherever I went

on the Riviera, I felt that nothing was as real as that book of flimsy paper. It loomed larger than the purple mountains, and its light was brighter than the light which flashes over the bays from the point of Cap Ferrat.

It was ubiquitous too. Which brings us back to the man at the bar. And, somewhat indirectly, to the Treasure Hunt.

III

He told me that his name was Smith. He was a frowsy little man of about forty-five, with a face tanned to the colour of Amontillado and wrinkled like a walnut. He was a gentleman, but a very shady gentleman. One felt that he was one of those unfortunates who leave London in a hurry, because of some little trouble in Hyde Park — one of those poor devils who are rather sillier than the rest of us, and suddenly have to resign from their clubs and live on a small allowance from a grudging relative. They all drift down to the Riviera sooner or later.

But they are not all theological scholars, like my friend. I have a fancy that he was a defrocked parson. Whatever he was, he seemed to have a considerable grievance against St. John, and not only against St. John but against all the gospels. Somehow or other he had wormed my business out of me — I was, indeed, not averse to talking about it — and he had discovered that for some months I had been engaged in an exhaustive study of the gospels.

This enraged him.

Did I know that Christ had megalomania, because he believed himself the Son of God; dromomania, because he could never stay in one place, but was always wandering about; sitiophobia, because he was forced to fast for forty days; and finally, obvious indications of insanity, as was witnessed by his cursing of the fig-tree when it would not bear fruit out of season? I told him that these long words meant very little to me, and added that if Christ was insane it was a pity that more people were not infected by his particular brand of insanity.

And then occurred a dialogue which somewhat disturbed me. For Mr. Smith suddenly mentioned something which had been at the back of my mind for a long time. It was an awkward problem with regard to the gospels from which, subconsciously, I had shied. We spoke as follows:

SMITH. I suppose you realize that all your gospel evidence is tainted?

MYSELF. Why?

SMITH. Because it's all written by believers.

MYSELF. Does that matter?

SMITH. It mightn't matter if there was any other sort of historical evidence to confirm it. *But there isn't!*

MYSELF. Yes, there is.

SMITH. What is it?

MYSELF (*a little awkwardly*). Really ... need we go into this? I don't think you're in quite a condition ...

SMITH. I'm not tight. It's you who're tight. With all these fairy tales. Come on, out with your evidence.

MYSELF. Very well. There's a sentence in Tacitus.

SMITH (*chuckling*). Oh, that old sentence in Tacitus!
The Christians are *so* proud of it. One little contemp-
tuous sentence from a Roman historian! One little sneer-
ing sentence to record the birth, life, teaching, death and
resurrection of the son of God! Otherwise ... nothing
(*he took another drink and smacked his lips*). Not a whisper!
Not a ripple! However, go on. Tell me your sentence.

I don't know why I didn't get up and walk away. It
would have been simpler. I think I was afraid that he
would cause a row of some sort. And so, I stayed.
I reminded him that Tacitus was writing of a sect who
are called 'Christians' by the common people of Rome,
as a term of reproach. He interrupted me.

SMITH. Yes, yes, I know all that. All I want to hear is
that sentence you're so proud of.
MYSELF. 'The originator of that name, one Christus,
had been executed in the reign of Tiberius by order of the
Administrator, Pontius Pilate.'[1]
SMITH. And that's all?
MYSELF. That's all. There are a few phrases of Sue-
tonius and Pliny the younger, but they don't help much.
SMITH. Otherwise you've only got the gospels?
MYSELF. Yes.
SMITH. Thank you very much. I hope you're satisfied.

And with that, to my great relief, he snorted, swallowed
his drink, and strolled away.
A few minutes later, I followed him. It was cold outside. Darkness was coming swiftly, and the wind was

[1] *Annals*, xv, 44.

rising. I remembered how Christ had once said, 'Yet a little while is the light with you. Walk while ye have the light, lest darkness come upon you . . .'[1]

But that, I felt, was rank sentimentality. It was also completely out of keeping with the spirit of honest research in which I was trying to work. And so I said to myself:

'Here we are, confronted by a fact which seems, on the face of it, to be very awkward. Let us sit down and think it out.'

I V

We have to face the almost incredible fact that, apart from the evidence of the gospels, and apart from that single sentence of Tacitus, *there is a complete lack of any historical testimony as to the very existence of Jesus.* Even more striking is the fact that there is also a complete lack of Jewish testimony. Consider Philo of Alexandria. He was born thirty-four years before the beginning of the Christian era. He died fifty-four years after it. We have over fifty works by him. In not one of them is there the smallest reference to Christ.

It is so astonishing that it looks almost like a conspiracy.

We stare once again at the sentence of Tacitus.

'The originator of that name, one Christus, was executed in the reign of Tiberius by order of the Administrator, Pontius Pilate.'

'Well, at least, that's something,' we mutter to our-

[1] St. John, xii, 35.

selves. 'Nobody has been able to deny the authenticity of this sentence in Tacitus.[1] I suppose we ought to be thankful for it. It's a voice from outside. A Pagan corroboration. And at least it fixes the date of the Crucifixion.'

But as we sit there, pondering, we realize that this little sentence does a good deal more than that. For men are not crucified for nothing. The sentence therefore implies some great offence against Roman authority. It also implies that this offence was of a nature which, for some extraordinary reason, caused it to be regarded by contemporaries as a great virtue. It implies even more than that. For Tacitus was writing about Nero and the burning of Rome, which occurred in July A.D. 64, and the sentence itself (as we ought to have pointed out before) occurs in a passage in which he relates how Nero tried to put the blame for the fire on to the Christians. And so, by implication, Tacitus is telling us that the execution of this 'one Christus', though it occurred in a completely obscure province, though it had a minimum of publicity, *though there was every conceivable reason why it should have been forgotten in a week*, was yet of so unusual a nature that Rome, the capital of the world, was echoing with the news of it, only a generation later.

That is what Tacitus is telling us. We have not read into his sentence a single implication that is not there.

[1] The distinguished critic, Charles Guignebert, Professor of the History of Christianity at the Sorbonne, who has devoted a lifetime to the task of tearing the gospels to shreds, mentions that some commentators have endeavoured to prove that even this little fragment of Tacitus is a late Christian interpolation. 'None of these critics has succeeded', he observes drily. So we may take it that Tacitus is reliable.

'All right,' says the Rationalist, 'we'll grant you these implications. It would be a shame to take away the one little straw out of which you've got to make so many bricks. But doesn't it strike you as rather pitiable that this God of yours should have been so very meagre with His evidence? Isn't He asking you to do an awful lot of work?'

We try to face this question honestly. It is a perfectly reasonable question. Shelley asked it, with considerable vehemence. In the notes to Queen Mab he says:

'Either the Christian religion is true, or it is false: if true it comes from God and its authenticity can admit of doubt and dispute no further than its omnipotent author is willing to allow. *Either the power or the goodness of God is called in question if He leaves those doctrines most essential to the well-being of man in doubt and dispute. If God has spoken, why is the universe not convinced?*'

v

This is a hurdle with a vengeance.

Can we jump it? And when I say jump, I mean jump, I don't mean 'dodge', or scramble round it with half-shut eyes. It is a tremendous hurdle, with countless rungs, and each rung is a problem.

There is the problem, for instance, of those vast portions of the human race who have never heard of Christ. Have you ever seen a picture of men and women bathing in the Ganges? The sacred river is black with them. It looks like a vast and somewhat unsavoury ant-heap. Are all those people damned? Will the breath of His scorn wither the densely populated plains of China? Will He pass by the aboriginals in Australia, the patient silly blacks with wide brown eyes, squatting under the gum-trees? Of all the immense and vividly painted procession of peoples who have danced round the earth, only a very few have ever heard of Christ.

Isn't that rather disturbing? Doesn't it seem, as Shelley said, as though God were either impotent to give His message as it should be given, or as though He did not care whether it were given or not?

Upon our answer, our *honest* answer to these questions, depends our future happiness.

Now, when one is puzzled about a man's motives, it is never a bad thing to put oneself in his shoes. Why was A so absurdly angry at our foolish little jest? Why was B so unreasonably happy at our foolish little compliment? Why is C afraid of meeting our friends? If you put yourself in his shoes, and if you know enough about him, you will see the reason for A's anger, B's joy, and C's fear. *Tout comprendre c'est tout pardonner* — which is one of the many eternal truths that spring up, like golden flowers, in the shadow of the cross.

It will probably be regarded as a piece of monstrous assumption if I suggest that we should put ourselves in God's shoes. There is obviously something vulgar about the phrase . . . I'm not denying it . . . it's an awful phrase. But when you are writing quickly, hot on the trail of an idea, you catch all sorts of trailing burrs and brambles which you can't brush off. If we were taking part in an academic procession, it would be different. But we're not. This is a treasure hunt.

And so, let us imagine, for a brief crazy moment, that we are God.

VI

We are omnipotent. The spheres obey us. We can make a bracelet of the stars, and string it round our wrist and toss it, like glittering dust, into the abyss. With a breath we can cause Infinity to blossom like a garden.

But such things, for the moment, are not our concern. Our Thought is on the earth — this little speck which (as we have seen) is particularly beloved by us.

Only a great poet could sustain such a flight of imagination. A poet like Francis Thompson, when he wrote:

> I fled Him, down the nights and down the days;
> I fled Him, down the arches of the years,
> I fled Him, down the labyrinthine ways
> Of my own mind; and in the mist of tears
> I hid from Him, and under running laughter.
> Up vistaed hopes I sped;
> And shot, precipitated,
> Adown Titanic glooms of chasmed fears,
> From those strong Feet that followed, followed after.

But we are not poets. We are only gentlemen of disbelief. No mystic nonsense for us. Our brains are clear, we are in full possession of our faculties, and we are faced with a perfectly simple problem. . . .

Why, if the Spirit of the Universe, whom we call God, chose to give through Christ a revelation of His purpose to the peoples of the earth, did He not give it with more authority and decision, and why did He not supply enough evidence to make it impossible for man to disbelieve?

Why does God allow doubt?

Why is His Revelation, if it be a revelation, still in question?

In other words, why doesn't He *tell* us, once again, and write it in letters of flame across the heavens? Why doesn't He say one word, one great thunderous Word across the bright cities of the world, and then leave us, secure in our belief, to worship Him?

Having asked these questions, we come once again to the task we faced a moment ago, of putting ourselves in God's shoes.

VII

We will assume that God decides to banish Doubt from the world.

We will assume that, once again, He sends His son in glory to the city, that on a winter's night there is a sudden radiance in the streets, a sudden hush in the business of men, whilst the waters of the river are stilled and a voice comes drifting from the stars.

What then?

Let us meet this immense conception with as prosaic and sober a mentality as possible. Let us see how the Rationalist would answer us. He would probably say:

'We will only answer your question "What then?" on the understanding that it is a rhetorical question, a sort of sublime joke. We know ... and we have a shrewd suspicion that you know too ... that such an event as you suggest is about as likely as the arrival of Santa Claus at the Savoy Hotel or the sudden appearance of Rip Van Winkle at the Bath Club. Still, we can imagine both these events, and we can also imagine the advent of Christ. But we must make it quite clear that we realize that we are imagining a fairy story.'

'Very well,' we reply. 'It doesn't matter in the least. Call it a fairy story, if you wish. We only want you to tell us what would happen to the world *if* the fairy story came true.'

To which the Rationalist would answer:

'If Christ came, as you suggest, one of two things would happen. The first, of course, is that the world would come to an end.'

'But supposing it *didn't*. Supposing Christ's advent were only a second revelation, a proof from God, once and for all, to modern civilization, that this *was* His son ... supposing it were His last means of dispelling all our doubt, what then?'

'Ah, I begin to see your point. Supposing there were a World without Doubt ...'

The Rationalist ponders. I do hope you will ponder too for a moment. Try to imagine what that world without doubt would be. Supposing he had come only for an hour. Science would have perpetuated that hour for all time. We should be able to see him on the cinema, to hear his voice on the gramophone. We should be able to read in the newspapers a thousand reports of his slightest gesture. There would not be the faintest shadow of a reason why any man or woman in any country in the world should for one moment question the complete authenticity of the Christian legend.

What then?

Ask yourself that question. Really ask yourself. And gradually, if you shut your eyes, and try to reason it all out, you will see a most tremendous paradox forming in your brain. The paradox is that the world, in the light of such a challenging revelation, would be a drab world, and that humanity would be infinitely the poorer. 'What!' you may exclaim, 'the world would be drab after Christ had shone in glory over the streets, and after we have had actual photographs of his presence, and records of his voice? Drab, when we couldn't help believing, even if we tried?'

Yes. Drab. But I do not think that word is quite strong enough. I think I should have said 'dead'.

VIII

Put it like this. If the Bible were as simple as, let us say, yesterday's issue of *The Times*, if we could personally consult the men who had written it, if we could go round the corner to a News Reel Theatre and see Christ raising Lazarus, if the whole thing were before our eyes — well, I can only repeat once more the 'rhetorical' question we asked the Rationalist, 'What then?'

All merit would have been taken from faith. All glory

from virtue. The man who did not do as Christ told him to do would be, quite frankly, a damned fool. And the man who *did* do what Christ told him to do would be no more admirable, and no more spiritually benefited, than the man who keeps within the speed limit and obeys the ordinary laws of the land.

In a World without Doubt, Christ would descend, with a dull and sickening thud, to the level of a policeman. He would be, at best, a sort of sublime magistrate.

That is the tremendous truth upon which, quite by accident, we have stumbled. I hope you will take that word 'stumbled' quite literally, because I am writing this book as I go along, feeling my way. I don't know what the last chapter will be, any more than you do. If I did know, the lust of the hunt wouldn't be in these pages.

However, we cannot realize how great that truth is unless we, once more, sum up our progress to date. We cannot have any idea of the heights we have reached unless we constantly pause, look back, and scan the ground which we have covered.

Our earth is unique in space — exit the fear of infinity.

Its guiding spirit is beneficent — exit the fear of death.

Man's appearance on earth was only yesterday, in the measurement of time — exit the fear of the vastness of Time.

If a son of God were to appear, he would presumably appear at about the time Christ appeared.

And . . .

If this revelation were to be of real value to man, in his climb upwards, *it would be a veiled revelation, a revelation which forced man to do his part and to share in the sacrifice.*

Let me make this last point quite clear.

The smallest acquaintance with Nature, the green-rimmed mirror in whose shadows we see the silver radiance of God's face, will inform us that all progress is the result of struggle. The survival of the fittest, which is so often quoted by the Rationalist as an example of God's callousness, can have a very different interpretation. It can suggest green leaves struggling upwards to the light, it can imply an amazingly delicate economy in which the chaff is sifted from the wheat, by immense and omnipotent hands.

Man, the highest creation of God, has never got 'something for nothing'. Throughout every hour of history he has had to fight. No sooner does he appear to have won a triumph over Nature than he is reminded that he cannot rest and that he has a long way further to go. In times of peace, on fertile plains, in hot climates, men have waxed fat and prosperous, and a fever comes to slay them. In times of plenty, when the world is running with gold, and the granaries are full, the men who should be friends stir up evil and fight, and the gold chokes them and the granaries are emptied. I often think that the last war may have been a supreme example of this sublime discipline. Men had been given power over the land and the sea and the air. In their hands were magic glasses which searched the secrets of the moon. They had learnt to speak across continents, their voices carried more swiftly and clearly than the shout of a full-throated giant. They had imprisoned the song of the nightingale on a disk of shining wax, they had set up screens in the dark on which, like strange ghosts, their women danced and loved, mystically evoked by a film of celluloid. Man was a great magician, yes! Heaven, it seemed, was in his grasp, as a bubble is in the grasp of a child. And then, like a spoilt child, he shattered it. The wreckage is still strewn around him.

History is a record of struggle. Progress is a parable of pain. And every spiritual adventure which has advanced the soul of man, has been a leap in the dark.

A leap in the dark! Isn't it possible that this is what we are asked to take? Isn't it extremely likely? Isn't it, in fact, the only way in which we *can* progress, in our spirits?

If we answer 'yes' we shall find that our answer fits in with everything that we have seen of nature or read of the struggles of man. It explains, with a sudden extraordinary radiance, the weird and almost incredible blank which we find about Christ in the pages of history.

To sum it all up, Doubt is the touchstone of a man's merit, the stepping stone on which he may 'rise from his dead self to higher things'.

And that, one realizes with a quick thrill of understanding, is why Christ so sternly and so frequently proclaimed the virtue of Faith.

IX

However, we are getting on too fast.

We are still for the purposes of argument gentlemen of disbelief, although we are in search of faith.

We are still on the Riviera, in spirit as well as in body.

True, we are somewhat less discouraged than before at the fact that, apart from the tiny sentence of Tacitus, history has spread so strange a cloak of darkness over the figure of Christ. For we feel it legitimate to presume that there is a divine purpose in this darkness. Yet even if we believe that our hope is *intended* to be only in the gospels, in the 'good news' (since Faith which contained no element of sacrifice would be without merit), we shall still find ourselves confronted by an enormous amount of discrepancies in the gospels themselves. And the gospels, we remember, are the documents where the clues for the treasure are hid.

We are now, indeed, at the darkest moment of our search.

Consider, for example, the question raised by my little friend in the cocktail bar, 'How do you get over St. John?' It will probably surprise many persons, who regard every word of the New Testament as equally valuable, to learn that for over a century even the most devout and earnest Christians have been seriously troubled about the gospel according to St. John. It seems incredible that Christians have not *always* been troubled. For instance, there is that little question of the raising of Lazarus. Why in the name of all that is holy did not any other of the gospels consider it worthy of mention, if it really happened? *Did it happen?* There is, again, the difficulty about the parables. Whether you have read the Bible recently or whether it is one of the books which you leave in the attic, you will remember, presumably, that Christ's main method of teaching was by parables. The parable of the foolish virgins, for example, is part of the common heritage of the civilized

European and so is the parable of the sower. Christ's parables, in fact, are among the most beautiful things about him — they are as fresh to-day as when they first sprang up, like lovely flowers, in the dusty deserts of theology. And needless to say, they still fall on deaf ears. But in the gospel according to St. John *there is not a single parable*.

Did you know that? And if you did, do you not agree that it is, to say the least of it, odd?

But these are not the most astonishing omissions.

There is no record of the Virgin Birth.

There is no record of the Temptation.

There is no record of the Transfiguration.

There is no Sermon on the Mount.

But there *is* an extremely long report, which is presumably intended to be regarded as verbatim, of what Christ said to his disciples during the last supper in the Upper Room. And nobody, in the days before short-hand was invented, could possibly have remembered all that speech.

All these difficulties, however, fade into insignificance by the side of the main problem, which is that Christ is apparently an utterly *different* Christ in St. John from the Christ of Matthew, Mark and Luke. Here is a Christ removed to an immense distance from the affairs of men, a Christ who seems to concern himself hardly at all with the little tiny details of our lives over which the other Christ lingered so lovingly. In the whole of St. John's Gospel the word 'mercy' does not appear. Nor the word 'compassion'. Nor the word 'forgiveness'. Christ does great works of mercy, it is true, but he prefaces them with such words as 'I must work the words of Him that sent me'. From the very outset he claims to be the Son of God, and his miracles are worked — unlike the miracles of the other gospels — with the clear object of substantiating this claim. 'The story in St. Matthew, St. Mark and St. Luke differs from this all along the line and, indeed, must appear to contradict it flatly by insisting that he positively forbade any sort of publication of the claim that he was the son of God'.[1]

X

If you are a man of Faith, do you find these problems disturbing, better left alone?

If you are a gentleman of disbelief, do you feel that we have at last plunged into a pit from which there is no means of extricating ourselves?

And if you are an ordinary reader, do you think that this discussion has gone on far too long, and that you would be better employed in reading something else?

Let me say a word to the 'ordinary reader'. Whoever you may be you can hardly fail to be interested in the treasure. Without it, you are a pitiable, powerless, worthless, decaying hulk of tissues and salts. With it, you are ageless, immensely important, and indestructible. Without it, you have every reason to be miserable, and if you blew your brains out nobody could possibly deny that you had every reason for doing so, and doing so at

[1] *According to Saint John*, Lord Charnwood, p. 120.

once. With it you have every reason to be happy, with a happiness greater than anything this world can offer.

And let me say another word. Up till now, the clues have led us closer and closer to the treasure. But being honest, we have faced all the difficult stumbling blocks. It may console the impatient to remind them that the gospel according to St. John is by far the most difficult stumbling block that we have encountered or that we *shall* encounter. It is the favourite target of every anti-Christian. It is, according to the Rationalist, the really weak spot in the whole Christian legend.

If, therefore, we can surmount this hurdle, we shall be almost in sight of the treasure.

And therefore, I hope, you will think it worth while to read on.

But *can* we surmount this hurdle?

The answer is yes.

XI

Yes!

I give that answer as soberly as if I were giving evidence on a matter of life and death in a Court of Law. And it is in the spirit of a Court of Law that I would ask you to read the gospel. You really *must* read it if you are to join in this detective hunt with me. Admittedly, it will be difficult for you to keep an entirely level head while reading it, because the sheer beauty of the prose will offer you as exciting an aesthetic experience as if you were listening to the D minor symphony of César Franck, or seeing, for the first time, the dim and unearthly grace of Giotto's frescoes in Padua.

However, read it under the hardest possible conditions, in your most embittered and incredulous mood, with a cigarette between your fingers and a whisky and soda by your side, convinced that the whole thing is a pious fraud. And whether you like it or not, you will be forced to certain very provoking conclusions.

The first conclusion at which you will arrive is that whoever wrote the gospel, with whatever object, was, at least, an *eye-witness* of the events he describes.[1] Over and over again there are little details, creeping in, glistening like tiny points of living gold on an ancient manuscript. And because these details are there, you have to ask *why* they are there. Are they the scrabblings of a madman? Are they included in order to substantiate a monstrous forgery? To perpetrate an immense practical joke of diabolical cruelty? The Rationalist, do not forget, has to presuppose that the author was either a madman, a forger, or a practical joker. Then let us ask the Rationalist which manner of man it was who wrote

'Let not your heart be troubled: ye believe in God, believe also in me. In my Father's house are many mansions: if it were not so, I would have told you. I go to prepare a place for you.'

Are those the words of a lunatic, a cheat, or a cad? You are forced to answer 'yes' if you deny that they are the words of Christ. Can you answer yes?

But to return to the details. I will give a few examples out of many.

[1] No serious scholar of Saint John can afford to neglect the brilliant analysis of this subject in *Religion and the New Testament* by R. H Malden. Oxford University Press, 1928.

Do you remember the story of the marriage in Cana? Jesus and his disciples were called to the marriage. His mother told him that there was no wine, but she added (in a curiously dramatic aside to the servants), 'Whatsoever he saith unto you, do it'.

The story goes on:

'And there were set there six water pots of stone, containing two or three firkins apiece. Jesus saith unto them, Fill the waterpots with water. And they filled them up to the brim. And he saith unto them, Draw out now, and bear unto the governor of the feast. And they bare it. When the ruler of the feast had tasted the water that was made wine, and knew not whence it was: (but the servants which drew the water knew) the governor of the feast called the bridegroom and saith unto him etc. etc.'

'Six water pots'. . . . 'two or three firkins' . . . 'but the servants knew' . . .

There are so many examples of this otherwise inexplicable inclusion of specific detail, that I will not weary you with them at length. 'Now there is at Jerusalem a pool called Bethesda, having *five porches*' — 'When therefore they had rowed *about five and twenty or thirty furlongs*' — 'When he had heard therefore that Lazarus was sick, he abode *two days* still in the same place where he was.'

These things may, of course, have been included to make the forgery more convincing. But why? Why forge at all? *Where is the motive?* The Rationalist must answer that question, before he tears up the gospel and condemns us to death.

XII

We are detectives, confronting the most disturbing mystery of the documents in which the treasure is hidden.

We take clues as they come.

The 'eye-witness' theory is interesting, but not particularly convincing. Here, however, suddenly thrust before us, is something which makes us sit up. It comes out of Hastings' *Dictionary of the Bible*. And it comes at a particularly happy moment for we have just remembered, rather poignantly, Dean Inge's assertion that the gospel represents 'free composition by the writer', and is not to be regarded as giving us the words of Christ. Is it possible that the Dean has been even more gloomy than was necessary? For in this Bible Dictionary is a little quiet piece of information which seems to me to explode like a bomb when you realize its significance. Here it is:

'*St. John puts into the lips of Christ no fewer than* 145 *words which he never uses in his own person.*'

'*Over* 500 *words which are freely used by St. John in his own portions of the Gospel are never once attributed by him to Christ.*'[1]

This is, indeed, a fact of quite exceptional significance. For the Rationalist, who maintains that the whole thing is a forgery, and the gloomy Dean, who maintains

[1] Hastings' *Dictionary of the Bible* (ii, 719). Quoted in *How to Understand the Gospels*, by Anthony Deane, a work of scholarship and spiritual beauty to which I owe a debt of deep gratitude.

that the whole thing is 'free composition', and implies that Christ never said the words attributed to him, are both forced into a position at least as difficult as that of the man of faith. They are both compelled to invent, out of the air, an unknown genius (for the gospel, at its lowest, is a superb work of art), who was also a forger of exceptional subtlety, and not only a forger, but a forger without any motive for forgery. Who, we may ask, *was* this singular person, this amazing artist, this wild lunatic, this unprincipled ruffian, this incredible compendium of virtue and vice?

'Very well,' says the Rationalist. 'You've got us there. We agree that our theories land us in just as many difficulties as yours. But that doesn't make *your* position any sounder. Even if we allow, for the purposes of argument, that the gospel really *was* written by St. John (which we still doubt), and that we *thought* he was writing the truth, how can you possibly maintain that the words are literally the words of Christ? Good Lord, man, there's one speech in it which goes on, with hardly a break, for nearly five chapters, about one hundred and fifty verses! Try writing out five verses of that, after reading it five times, and see what happens! And even if you got *them* fairly right you'd still have done only a thirtieth of them! The only way you can make your theory work is to suggest that St. John was an expert stenographer, which would probably strike you as irreverent.'

We pause and think.

The words of Christ, or the words of — someone else?

The words of God, or the words of man?

It makes a difference. Countless men and women,

throughout the generations, have received infinite comfort by repeating those words, feeling that they came from a divine source. Have they all been fooled? Would it have been just the same for them if they had repeated, let us say, the sonnets of Shakespeare?

Once again the hurdle seems insurmountable.

XIII

Let us pause for a minute, while I tell you a story.

A good many years ago, when I was a reporter, I was suddenly packed off to interview Lord —— about some political matter.

Before leaving I looked him up in *Who's Who*, and discovered that he had held a position of considerable importance in the days of Disraeli, and was now nearly ninety. Having had a certain experience of interviewing very old men I did not look forward to the task with very much pleasure. All that one usually managed to extract was a series of rather poignant grunts, which one had to interpret, according to one's editorial policy, in terms of condemnation, or approbation, of the Modern Girl.

However, orders are orders, so I set off, and duly arrived at an exquisite Queen Anne house. After being snubbed by the butler, I was shown in to see his lordship, and at first my worst fears seemed to be confirmed. For though nobody could have been more charming or more courteous, his mind was quite evidently elsewhere. It was, in fact, solely absorbed in the destruction of flies. He wandered about the room with a dreadful little wire contraption, murmuring 'yes' or 'no', at random, and the only answer he gave to my questions was an ineffective little bang on the glass.

And then, quite suddenly, he paused, against the sunlit window. A light came into his eyes. His voice gathered power. 'I remember a speech by Disraeli', he muttered. He cleared his throat. He began to repeat the speech. He went on for nearly ten minutes. It was an astonishing feat. And then equally suddenly, he stopped, sank on to the window seat, and lifted a feeble hand to flick a fly.

'And what,' you may ask, 'has all this to do with the gospel according to St. John?'

It has this to do with it. St. John was a very old man when the gospel was first given to the world. And I want you to ask yourself whether it is so impossible to attribute the discrepancies in this gospel to the wanderings of an old man's memory. Old men's minds work in a mysterious way. They get muddled about dates (as St. John constantly did), but they remember vivid little details. They forget enormously important events, but they can recall things that people said to them, with the authenticity of a gramophone record. Besides, there is the possibility, which the Rationalist always ignores, that St. John took notes. It is only a theory, but it is not a very unreasonable theory. However, even if he was relying on his memory, was the feat he achieved, of recalling Christ's discourse during the Last Supper, so utterly impossible? The occasion was fraught with tragedy. It was a moment unique in the history of the world. The wings of death were darkening the room, and there was a silence like the silence that comes before a storm. Through that silence came a voice, speaking words whose like had never been heard before on this earth. Is it not possible that, even if we deny all supernatural explanations, those words may not have been burned, as with an immortal brand, upon the disciple's brain? For you must remember that John was the disciple 'whom Jesus loved'.

If he was *not*, he was the mysterious genius-cum-lunatic-cum-forger which the Rationalist is compelled to invent.

Which was he?

You do not know. But you *do* know that from his pen came the words 'Little children, yet a little while I am with you. Whither I go, ye cannot come; so now I say to you, A new commandment I give unto you, That ye love one another, as I have loved you.'

Lunatic? Forger? Well . . .

XIV

This discussion threatens to be interminable.

We will therefore stop it.

However, I hope that you yourself may feel inclined to pursue it, in the privacy of your own homes, because, apart from all other considerations, you will find it the most exciting sort of detective story, a detective story in real life, with an immense prize waiting for you, and any number of clues, stacked in all the big public libraries.

I have examined as many of those clues as was in my power — I think I have read and annotated upwards of twenty books on St. John's Gospel — and the more I read, the more I was convinced that St. John was the author and that a divine truth was in him.

You will find many glib people who will tell you that a Galilean fisherman would be quite incapable of writing such profound philosophy. They are the same sort of people who tell you that Shakespeare could not have written *Hamlet*.

You will find — but I promised to draw a line, and leave you to continue the search for yourselves. I will keep that promise. And all I would say, before leaving you, is this: 'Don't forget that St. John is the *biggest* hurdle. If we can surmount that, the treasure is practically ours.'

I myself surmounted it, loaded as I was with a heavy burden of incredulity, prejudice, and active hostility. It was almost as if I were pushed over the hurdle against my will, not by the force of faith but by the force of accumulated fact.

If you would care to see what other hurdles are waiting for us, and how we may, or may not, surmount them, I should be delighted if you would accompany me. But I fear that we shall have to wait till the next chapter, for this discussion has already gone on far too long.

In the meantime, however, I want to add a little Epilogue. It might be entitled 'A Few Words to a Great Critic'.

XV

Up till now, I hope you will admit, we have been extremely lenient with those learned gentlemen who, at every twist and turn, have endeavoured to dissuade us from our hunt for the treasure.

To please them, we have called outselves 'gentlemen of disbelief', for indeed, that is what we still are. We have listened to their most disturbing arguments. We have not endeavoured to shirk a single one of their theories. But occasionally, we find them — to be quite frank — a little tedious. We will tell them why.

And in order that nobody may accuse us of being pusillanimous, we will single out for our attentions the most distinguished of these gentlemen who exists in the modern world, none other than the Professor of the History of Christianity in that most learned of universities, the Sorbonne. His name is Professor Charles Guignebert.

Now Professor Guignebert is the 'big noise' of Rationalism. What he does not know about destructive criticism is not worth knowing. He has put his head through every hole in the Bible and wriggled it about, to the infinite satisfaction of the crowd. But I am going to suggest that though it is a very remarkable head, stuffed with facts, dates, numbers and theories, though it may rival the head of Mr. H. G. Wells' Grand Lunar in acumen and erudition, it is a head which contains the most peculiar gaps.

I will give you an example of what I mean in a moment, but I would first pause to suggest that if such an important head, so lavishly crowned and so largely venerated, contains such gaps, it is reasonable to suppose that the other Rationalists, who circle round the Grand Lunar's throne, may contain even graver deficiencies.

Now for the gap in question.

At the end of a chapter of brilliant destructive criticism of the whole history of Christ,[1] he suddenly asks this question — a question so naive that it takes the breath away:

'*Lacking the help of the historical life of Jesus is there at least a possibility of arriving at some knowledge of his character and his fundamental ideas?*'[2]

He adds that he does not always see in the sayings ascribed to Jesus the 'originality which is sometimes ascribed to them'.

He concludes by observing that 'many of these sayings would attract no attention whatever if they had been found in some dubious collection of *agrapha* instead of in a canonical book'.

As soon as I read that sentence I reached for the Bible. It fell open at the sixth chapter of St. Luke. I read:

'Love your enemies, do good to them which hate you, Bless them that curse you, and pray for them which despitefully use you. And unto him that smiteth thee on the one cheek offer also the other, and him that taketh away thy cloke forbid not to take thy coat also.'

[1] *Jesus*, by Charles Guignebert, with an Introduction by S. H. Hooke, Samuel Davidson Professor of Old Testament Studies in the University of London (Kegan Paul).
[2] Ibid.

It is lucky I opened the Bible at that passage, because otherwise I might have been tempted to smite the Professor on both cheeks. As it is, the nearest approach I can make to loving him is to limit my antagonism to a mild sarcasm.

I do not know if this is one of the sayings of Jesus in which the learned Professor of the Sorbonne can see no 'originality'. To me it seems original enough, and so daringly modern that it is a good deal in advance of any of the programmes of the advanced Left in any part of the world. Nor can I judge whether it 'would attract no attention whatever if it had been found in some dubious collection of *agrapha*'. I don't know much about dubious collections of *agrapha*, and I don't want to.

But I do know that when Jesus made this supposedly unoriginal and tedious remark, he made it at a time when the rabbis, the recognized guardians of learning, spent their entire lives in splitting hairs on piffling little points of doctrine, in poring over minute details of procedure, in growing blind and bald and deaf in their scrabblings after the dead perfection of orthodoxy. I also know that the gospels which enshrine his sayings 'date from an age when religious writing was almost invariably prolix and diffuse.' They come from Orientals, who with any unusual experience to relate, loved to set it forth at vast length, and with wearisome insistence upon its unique character. But the Evangelists are masters of clarity and precision.[1]

'*Love your enemies, do good to them that hate you, Bless them that curse you . . .*'

[1] *How To Understand the Gospels*, Anthony Deane (Hodder & Stoughton)

'Unoriginal?' Well, Professor, it is so original that the world has not yet been able to summon up the courage to obey it.

However, the Professor's most urgent, and, if we are being frank, most unintelligent question, is whether there may not be at least a possibility of arriving at some knowledge of Jesus' character and his fundamental ideas. I simply cannot refrain from saying that this question strikes me as downright silly. The Professor implies that what we know of Christ's character in the gospels is a hotch-potch of legend, a cloudy invention of some bemused peasants, and all he will admit, in his most generous moment, is that 'the outline of a man and the traces of an individual activity are still to be distinguished'.

Ye gods! If you have ever done any writing you may have a faint idea of the immense difficulty of making a character *live* even for a single publishing season, in a single language. And if you have ever done any reading, the remotest acquaintance with European literature will inform you that there are no 'characters', not even Don Quixote (the most lifelike evocation of an individual in literature) which are more than tiny shadows against the immense reality of the character of Jesus.

You cannot deny the reality of this character, *in whatever body it resided*. Even if we were to grant the Professor's theory that it is all a hotch-potch of legend, *somebody* said 'The Sabbath was made for man, and not man for the Sabbath'; *somebody* said 'For what shall it profit a man if he shall gain the whole world and lose his own soul'; *somebody* said 'Suffer the little children to come unto me, and forbid them not: for of such is the Kingdom of God'; *somebody* said 'How hardly shall they that have riches enter into the Kingdom of God'; *somebody* said 'All they that take the sword shall perish with the sword'.

Somebody said these things, because they are staring me in the face at this moment from the Bible. And whoever said them was *gigantic*. And whoever said them was *living*, because we are in the year 1936 and I am 'modern' and you are 'modern', and we both of us like going to the cinema and we can both drive a car and all that sort of thing, and yet we cannot find in any contemporary literature any phrases which have a shadow of the beauty, the truth, the individuality, nor the *indestructibility* of those phrases.

And remember, I have only quoted five sentences at random.

Read those sentences again. And then repeat once more the little querulous question of the Professor. 'Is there a possibility of arriving at some knowledge of His character?'

Yes, Professor, there is a possibility of arriving at some knowledge of his character. But in order to arrive at it you will have to take your eye from the microscope, and look out of your window, to the stars.

CHAPTER IV

MESSIAH OR MAGICIAN?

I

THE title of this chapter is dramatic, but it is hardly as dramatic as the subject.

You and I are at a turning point in our lives. We have come a long way. We set out, in our search for Faith, armed with nothing but a microscope, a tape-measure, and a determination not to be fooled.

When we started, we had little hopes of reaching our goal. Our very instincts rebelled against the thoughts of such a possibility. We were frightened, desperately in awe of the cruel regalia of the stars. We wanted to escape from the accusing finger of Eternity. But wherever we turned to escape we found mist, and veil after veil of Nothingness. Athwart the most distant veil there glimmered a sign which looked curiously like a cross. We began to walk towards it, certain that it would prove to be a mirage. But it did not prove to be a mirage. It became more and more solid. We are not yet in its shadow, but we can begin to discern the outlines of the figure that is stretched upon it.

And remember, we have got thus far by following the historical facts. We have consistently looked on the worst side of the picture. We have not abandoned ourselves to any mystical ecstasies. When we felt them approaching we ran away. We sniffed no incense. We lit a cigarette. Perhaps our fingers were trembling. That doesn't matter. We lit it. We drank no heady wine of theology — we ordered another cocktail. We sought no cloisters — we went to the Riviera. And as I wrote that last sentence, I realized that unwittingly I had clumsily paraphrased, once again, Francis Thompson's immortal *Hound of Heaven:*

> I pleaded, outlaw-wise,
> By many a hearted casement, curtained red,
> Trellised with intertwining charities;
> (For though I knew His love Who followed,
> Yet I was sore adread
> Lest, having Him, I must have naught beside).
> But, if one little casement parted wide,
> The gust of His approach would clash it to.
> Fear wist not to evade, as Love wist to pursue.

And *still* we flee. We are determined to kick against the pricks until the last minute.

It is really very important that we should realize this. We are in the position of men who are taking a cure with the positive conviction that it is going to do no good. There is nothing of the Lourdes mentality about us. And that is why it is so remarkable that, in spite of ourselves, we have been pushed, forced, impelled, guided, use what word you will, to the very foot of the cross.

The figure on the cross gradually becomes real to us. We lower our eyes. We will not look, not yet. We have still to fumble with a lot of manuscripts, stare at a number of ancient documents through the microscope. Somehow we can't do that, so close to the cross. We feel a little uneasy.

So let us retreat a little.

That's better. We are once again in the shadows. Once again we are gentlemen of disbelief.

'The figure *may* be false,' we mutter to ourselves. 'We mustn't get absurd ideas into our heads. It may be only a pious Image.'

An Image?

With that word 'image' ringing in our ears, I would ask you to read with me a few sentences from a very wise book.[1] Here they are:

'Great numbers of ordinary readers have derived a knowledge of Jesus Christ amounting to what, though my own phrase jars on me a little, I can only call personal acquaintance. This sense of acquaintance with His person really far exceeds anything similar that we possess in regard to any other historical figure. In occasional moments of confidence two of us could discuss together what Jesus Christ would have said or done in any given circumstances. We should do so with a reality of interest, and what is more, with a prospect of fairly definite result, to which there is certainly no parallel.'

'Don't listen to him,' we mutter to ourselves. 'Lord Charnwood is talking through his hat.'

Is he?

Read on:

'If corroboration is wanted for the idea which we thus draw from the Gospels, corroboration is ready. In early

[1] *According to Saint John*, Lord Charnwood.

writers so different as Clement of Rome, St. James, the author of the Epistle to the Hebrews, St. Peter, the author of the Acts, and St. Paul, we find concordant testimony to what might loosely be called the Christian rule of conduct accepted *from the first*. The traits of this pattern are those of the *historic* Jesus. The pattern has this utterly singular feature: it is originally the type of a man with the intellect and temperament of genius, and with will and nerves of steel, engaged upon a strange, tremendous enterprise, *yet it is without hesitation taken home for personal use by people, whom differences of intelligence, temperament, circumstances, vocation, strength, race, age, sex, would seem to place immeasurably far from Him.*'

'An Image?' we ask the Rationalist.

'Yes,' he replies somewhat testily. 'Based upon a man, of course, but absurdly touched up.'

'Touched up? I see. You mean, he was just a man. He couldn't, for example, work a miracle?'

'Good God, no,' grunts the Rationalist. 'Look at the silly sort of miracles they said he *did* work. That ought to be enough for you!'

'All right. We'll look at them.'

And so, once more, out with our microscopes. They look rather feeble, these little lenses, in the curious radiance which is gathering round us. Still, they are the best, the most powerful, the most modern microscopes, that we can buy. We level them over the gospel miracles.

A good writer, I suppose, ought not to have to remind his readers that drama is in the air. It ought to be implicit in his phrases.

But I can't help standing back, for a moment, in order to remark how extremely exciting this moment is. For, in the documents before us, there *may* be something overwhelming, there *may* be the true gold of wisdom. No, that is not what I *meant* to say at all. What I meant was that there may be certain things which can only be explained by God.

There may be, in the gospels, an accumulation of finely-sifted historical evidence which, in spite of all the frenzied efforts of the Rationalists, turn the Ghost Stories into legally attested evidence, and transmute the pious fictions into sober facts.

There *may* be this evidence.

If there is — however, it is too early to think about that. If there is, our whole lives, obviously, will be given a revolutionary switch. We don't feel prepared for that, just yet.

But we *are* — well — rather excited.

III

We will begin by assuming that all the miracles are fakes.

We will glide gracefully over the reason why they are

faked. We will ignore the somewhat potent questions which the men of faith might put to us, such as '*why* these monstrous lies? *Why* these fantastic and ingenious conceits? *Why* should uneducated peasants suddenly conceive such astonishing illusions, and why should they persist in these illusions to the point of death?'

We don't know why. We are gentlemen of disbelief, bless us. We are not concerned with motives. All we know is that miracles don't happen.

The miracles, therefore, are fakes.

How can we prove it?

Well, obviously, there is one way, which should make a particular appeal to the legally minded. We can endeavour to show proof of conspiracy, of illicit collaboration between the writers. It is hardly conceivable that a number of forgers, who were endeavouring to foist a colossal illusion upon the world, should not take the elementary precaution of seeing that their stories tallied. They were men, if we are to believe the critics, of astonishing acumen, boundless invention, and inexhaustible cunning. They had every opportunity to conspire. Even if they had not done so, the early church could have 'cooked' their stories for them. Let us examine the evidence of this conspiracy.

Consider the resurrection of the daughter of Jairus. It is a very important miracle. If the account of it is faked we may be quite certain that all the stories will tally. There will be a smoothing out of any discrepancies. Well . . .

According to Mark, Jairus, who was one of the rulers of the synagogue, came hurrying to Jesus, fell at his feet, and besought him saying 'My little daughter lieth at the point of death'. And on the way to Jairus's house some people met them saying "Thy daughter is dead. Why troublest thou the Master any further?'

According to Matthew, on the other hand, Jairus came to him, worshipped and said 'My daugher is *even now dead*: but come and lay thy hand upon her and she shall live'.

And Luke differs once again. For he does not tell us whether Jairus said the daughter was dead or dying. He only says that he fell down at Jesus' feet and besought him to come to his house.

Conspiracy? Collaboration?

Well, no. Not exactly. We shall have to give up *that* argument. Of course you can say that this discrepancy disproves the truth of the whole story. But it is a very minor discrepancy compared with the facts upon which all the stories are agreed, namely that the daughter *was* raised from the dead, and that when Jesus came into the house he said the quiet but stupendous words 'She is not dead but sleepeth'.

As gentlemen of disbelief we are therefore faced with a very awkward dilemma in the very first miracle we hit upon. (We chose it, by the way, because it is triumphantly cited by Professor Guignebert, the Solomon of the Sorbonne, to prove that all the miracles are a lot of hotch-potch.) The dilemma is that if the writers of the New Testament were forgers they were extremely clumsy and simple men to leave such an obvious hole in the fabric of their forgery. And yet, though they were so clumsy and simple they managed to invent a superb story, culminating in a dramatic climax with the words 'She is not dead but sleepeth', words which have rung through the world ever since.

We hate to admit it but the three stories, taken together, have a ring of truth more convincing than if they had all said exactly the same thing. Supposing three witnesses were telling the story of an accident in our own time. A boy, we will say, has just been rescued from the river. The father runs to the doctor, crying to him to come and give artificial respiration. Smith might swear that the father said 'My boy's drowned'. Jones might swear that the father said 'My boy's nearly drowned'. Robinson might not be sure what the father said at all. *But*, if Smith Jones and Robinson had thrown the boy into the pond themselves, and had then gone to the doctor's to establish an alibi, you may be pretty certain that their stories would be the same to the smallest detail.

I have dealt with this miracle at a certain length because it is typical of many miracles in the New Testament. There *are* little discrepancies. As gentlemen of disbelief we are assuming that these discrepancies invalidate the miracles. But if we do that, we have to acquit the writers of any sort of conspiracy.

Well — the air is slightly cleared.

I V

The miracles are fakes. Of that we are assured.

All we have been forced to admit, so far, is that they are *honest* fakes, if you will forgive the lapse into Irish.

135

Now let us revert, once more, to the *a priori* method.

We assumed, firstly, that men inventing a miracle would see that the details tallied. The details didn't tally. So we gave up that line of approach.

We will now assume, secondly, that men inventing a miracle would very scrupulously avoid mentioning any persons who might deny the miracle. For we must remember that when the gospels were first given publicity the whole of the Holy Land abounded with persons who must have been eye-witnesses of the main incidents of Christ's career. True, these persons were getting on in years, but they were not so far gone that their memories were defunct nor their tongues paralysed. In other words, there was a very considerable body of *living* testimony with which the writers of the gospels had to contend.

We must therefore, as gentlemen of disbelief, expect that these miracles which we are about to investigate will all be of an entirely vague and shadowy nature. We must take it for granted, that names, dates, places will not be mentioned. The forgers may be unscrupulous but they are not fools. If I say that once, in a dark lane, I encountered a ruffian of Herculean strength and knocked him flat with the palm of my hand, nobody can contradict me, though many might regret such an unwonted departure from my pacific protestations. But if I say that on April 1st, 1936, I met Carnera opposite 195 Bond Street, and tossed him lightly through the door of the Embassy Club, into the lap of the Viscountess Castlerosse, that is, as they say, *autre chose*. Quite a number of people could politely differ from this statement, including Carnera himself.

Well, what do we find in the New Testament miracles?

To our disgust, we find that these wretched forgers who invented these tiresome stories are constantly putting in the most embarrassing circumstantial details. They really might have had more consideration for future generations of sceptics. Why, for instance, should they write fiction about Jairus, of all people? Jairus was a ruler of the synagogue. An important man. It is fairly safe to assume that he had dozens of garrulous relations. Why should the inventors of this miracle have mentioned him by name, knowing only too well that he could rise up and point a finger of indignation at them and say 'What is all this nonsense? My daughter was never ill. I never heard of Jesus Christ. How dare you spread these stories?'

And why, again, should they hit on the miracle of Malchus? He was a servant of the High Priest. Anybody could identify him. They said that his ear had been cut off and that Christ healed it. That is a very odd thing even to *think* about a man, let alone to write, if it never happened. The inventors of these stories must have had the most extraordinary minds. And why Lazarus, who was known to hundreds of people? And why, as we are facing up to the most stupendous lies of all, the feeding of the five thousand? This story was being calmly and concisely handed round, on slips of parchment, as a *fact*, to the general public. If it was a lie, or an invention, can any amount of credulity, Eastern mysticism, or any of the other explanations with which the higher critics entrench themselves against the thunders of God, explain the daring effrontery of the men who circulated that story? 'All right — it's only twenty years ago . . . where *are* these five thousand? They can't all be dead.' That is the first criticism that would greet the man who had invented that story.

No. They weren't all dead. That is an historical fact. And these stories *were* circulating. That is another historical fact. Where do those two historical facts lead us?

If we were *not* gentlemen of disbelief they might lead us to the fact that, at the very time that the first legend of this miracle was being handed round, on those pieces of parchment, there were still many men and women walking the dusty streets, whose bodies had once been nourished by a strange bread, that was not as the bread of this world.

v

'But this is ridiculous!' we exclaim. 'Think of it *happening*. Don't go off into a lot of second-rate prose about "strange bread". *Think* of it happening. A Jew, in a long dusty robe, sitting on the grass, and breaking bread. Five loaves. And he goes on breaking bread. And one loaf springs out of another, and so on, and so on. It's too idiotic. Somebody invented it.'

'Why?'

'I don't know. But a thing like that can't happen.'

'Then why did they say it happened, at the top of their voices, when so many people could contradict them?'

'I tell you I don't know. But religious hysteria can be responsible for anything. It makes people feel comfortable.'

'Does it make people feel comfortable to be crucified upside down?'

'What the devil . . . ?'

'That's what happened to St. Peter. That was the reward for spreading stories like this. Why then did they spread them?'

'Oh, go away. You make me tired.'

That fragment of dialogue, between a man of faith and a gentleman of disbelief, is not without reality. And since it illuminated the main thesis of the gentleman of disbelief, which may be described as 'I don't believe in miracles, even if I see them', I would like to give my flimsy arguments a momentary weight by calling the evidence of Sir Oliver Lodge on the whole question of miracles in general. He is answering a gentleman called Professor Tyndall, who observed: 'Science asserts that no prayers avail to call showers from heaven or deflect towards us a single beam of the sun, without a disturbance of natural law of a very serious nature.'

Sir Oliver replies:

'The assertion is that any act, if achieved *by the special volition* of the Eternal, would be a miracle.'

He continues:

'The implied *dogma* is that the special volition of the Eternal cannot, or at any rate does not, accomplish anything whatever in the physical world.'

Sir Oliver, after pointing out that this dogma is not a deduction from any of the known principles of physical science, observes, 'The alleged unscientific character of prayer for rain depends really not upon its conflict with any known physical law, since it need involve no greater interference with the order of nature than is implied in a request to a gardener to water the garden. Nor does it really depend upon the impossibility of causing rain to fall when otherwise it would not. It depends upon the disbelief of "science" *in any power who can and will attend and act.*'

I have quoted this passage in order to refute the many loose-thinking persons who blandly state that a miracle is an interference with the laws of nature. It is only an interference with the laws of nature if you believe that the Universe is a blind machine, started by Nobody, attended by Nobody, interested in Nobody, a machine, none the less, with incredibly complicated laws (drawn up by Nobody), and a machine which, though it is a mass manufacturer of souls does not possess a Soul itself, because it is Nobody.

And if you believe that, you will believe anything.

V I

However, we are getting on too fast. We must hurry back to our sceptic's tea-party.

The miracles are fakes. Nothing will budge us from that conviction. All that we will admit is that firstly, they are 'honest' fakes, because we found very definite evidence that the writers did not conspire together, and secondly that they are very *daring* fakes, because the writers kept on mentioning persons and places. We feel rather annoyed by the fact that we are unable to produce a scrap of historical evidence to show that a single person contradicted any of these wild lies. We can only assume that the lies were so far-fetched that nobody bothered.

However, as we continue the examination of these pious forgeries, our amazement at the ingenuity of the forgers increases. If they had been writing with the one object of confounding us poor Rationalists, they could not have done it better. For not only is it astonishing that they were able to invent such stories, but it is even more astonishing that they were able to *refrain* from inventing other stories.

Do you know the Christ of the Apocrypha? Most people don't. He is a very miraculous person indeed. Far more miraculous than the Christ we know. He is, of course, entirely the product of pious early Christians, whose minds were so inflamed by the legend of the true Christ that they wove round him haloes of their own invention . . . haloes which became him not at all.

The Apocrypha *is* fiction. And listen to the sort of fiction it is! I will give two extracts, both of them from the spurious gospel of Thomas, which is supposed to give the story of Christ's childhood.

'The little child Jesus, when he was five years old, was playing at the ford of a brook. And having made soft clay he fashioned thereof twelve sparrows. And it was the Sabbath day when he did these things. And Joseph came to the place and cried out to him saying, Wherefore doest thou these things on the Sabbath which it is not lawful to do? But Jesus clapped his hands together and cried out to the sparrows and said to them "Go!" and the sparrows took their flight and went away chirping.'

This is certainly a remarkable performance. Mr. Maskelyne could not better it. Moreover, it is a completely pointless performance. It does nobody any good. It illustrates no moral. It is only a rather tiresome exhibition of a small boy 'showing off'.

Therefore, as Rationalists, we are compelled to exclaim, 'How very clever of the men who invented the gospel miracles to avoid mentioning such miracles as that! And what real genius these unscrupulous forgers manifested in the story they *did* make up about Christ and the Sabbath.'

Do you remember that story? Christ had entered the synagogue on a Sabbath. There was a man there who had a withered hand. The Pharisees watched, to see if he would heal the man, so that they might accuse him of breaking the Sabbath.

'And he saith unto the man which had the withered hand, Stand forth. And he saith unto them, Is it lawful to do good on the Sabbath day, or to do evil? To save life or to kill? But they held their peace. And when he had looked round about on them with anger, being grieved for the hardness of their hearts, he saith unto the man, Stretch forth thine hand. And he stretched it out; and his hand was restored whole as the other.'

Marvellous apostles! Not only do they invent a superb lie but they attach to that lie (and to every other miracle) an equally superb system of ethics! Marvellous apostles! They were so cunning, so far-seeing, that they made Christ work his miracles *only* in order to point a moral and illustrate his teaching. How very much cleverer they were than the silly people who wrote the Apocrypha! Which reminds me that there is one other little extract from the spurious gospel of Thomas which we should consider:

'Jesus went through the village, and a child ran and dashed against his shoulder. And Jesus was provoked and said unto him Thou shalt not finish thy course. And immediately the child fell down and died.'

Can you imagine, for a single instant, Christ performing a miracle like that? No, you can't. Why not? The man of Faith *might* answer 'Because Christ was a real person and because we know that the truth about his life is told in the New Testament and nowhere else'. The Rationalist *must* answer, 'Because the men who invented the miracles were exceptionally clever. They would not allow any discrepancies of that nature ... any flaws.'

To which the man of faith retorts, 'But we've already seen that they *did* allow discrepancies and flaws. You can't have it both ways.'

And the Rationalist snaps, 'You make me tired. And anyway, you were silly to quote the Apocrypha, even though you agree that it *is* a forgery. Because it's an example of the absurd way in which fantastic legends spring up about any prophet. And I'd bet you anything you like that if you took the gospels in the order in which they were written you'd find that the last gospel had a great many more miracles added to it than the first.'

'How much did you say you'd bet?'

'Well ... what are you getting at?'

'How much?'

'I thought this was a religious discussion,' sniffs the Rationalist.

VII

It is a religious discussion. And the Rationalist has put his foot into it rather badly.

He is quite right in saying that, since we know the miracles to be fakes, we should be justified in assuming that the stories would grow more and more elaborate with each gospel, that the miracles would become more and more numerous.

Unfortunately for the Rationalist, however, exactly the opposite is the case. The greatest number of miracles, per page, occurs in the first gospel of all, which is the gospel according to St. Mark. And there is another thing which, as detectives, cannot fail to excite us, however much we may regret it, as gentlemen of disbelief. Namely, that this gospel of St. Mark is the only gospel which admits that *there were occasions on which Christ could not do any miracles at all!* The other apostles, presumably, refrained from such an admission because they thought it would be dangerous, in view of the storms which were threatening the early Church.

Incredibly subtle St. Mark! Not only did he forge and concoct the most fantastic legends, but in order to make these legends more convincing, he puts in a passage to say that Christ could not *always* do as he wished — he was only human after all. And not only does he hit upon this brilliant invention, but he prefaces it with one of the best epigrams of ancient or modern times (all out of his own simple head). He invents the epigram, 'A prophet is not without honour, save in his own country'. And then, he adds, 'And he could there do no mighty work, save that he laid his hands upon a few sick folk'.

And now we must really admit that as gentlemen of disbelief we are finding our rationalism demands of us almost as much credulity as the Christian's faith. How *are* we to continue our assumption that all these miracles and these subtleties and these devices came out of the head of a simple peasant? Well, we *do* believe it. Miracles don't happen, we know that. All the same, we are bound to admit a grudging praise to this man Mark, merely because he was such a superb literary artist.

Think of this story, then, in terms of literature alone. 'He could there do no mighty work . . .'

Christ snubbed, Christ trying and failing — yes, Christ *failing* — does not this admission make the story of the other miracles even more remarkable? If Mark had left out that part of the story, if he had told a story of unbroken triumph and unflagging power, the story would be infinitely the poorer.

It needs only a little imagination to conjure up for ourselves a picture of sick who were brought to him and sent away as bad as they came, of women who were *not* healed, of devils who were not cast out, but raged before him triumphantly, while the wretched men whom they tormented cried and spat and blasphemed, dancing before him with obscene gestures in the eastern sunlight, while he stared at them with wide, sorrowful eyes, unable to help them.

VIII

All this is very unsatisfactory.

For though we know the miracles are fakes, we are being gradually driven into the singular position that in order to prove the falsity of one miracle we have to believe in another. In order to prove that Christ's miracles did *not* happen we have to prove that another very definite miracle did happen — the miracle of the stories themselves.

I will make this point absolutely clear, not by reiterating the remarkable cumulative evidence which we have already collected, but by asking you to consider only one of Christ's miracles. The case of the woman who was healed of an issue of blood.

I will preface this case by a few questions to a Rationalist.

QUESTION. You agree that the gospels were written in the first century A.D.?

ANSWER. Well . . .

QUESTION. It doesn't matter. Say that they were written somewhere in the first *five* centuries A.D., if you like. Will you grant us *that*?

ANSWER. Of course.

QUESTION. If we can produce from these documents a story which anticipates medical science by over a thousand years. . . .

ANSWER. What do you mean? 'Anticipates medical science?' Some vague hotch-potch about the soul's effect on the body?

QUESTION. No. Nothing at all vague. A concise description of a physical function which was completely unrecognized by medical science even in the eighteenth century.

ANSWER. In the New Testament?

QUESTION. Certainly. And not particularly emphasized, either. Thrown in quite casually.

ANSWER. You can't produce it.

QUESTION. Can't we? All right. Read this!

We hand him the Bible. He reads. Will you read too? It is the fifth chapter of the gospel according to St. Mark. And as we are detectives, I would ask you to pay particular attention to detail.

'And much people followed him, and thronged him. And a certain woman, which had an issue of blood twelve years, and had suffered many things of many physicians, and had spent all that she had, and was nothing bettered, but rather grew worse, When she had heard of Jesus, came in the press behind, and touched his garment. For she said, If I may touch but his clothes, I shall be whole. And straightway the fountain of her blood was dried up; and she felt in her body that she was healed of that plague. And Jesus, immediately knowing in himself that virtue had gone out of him, turned him about in the press, and said, Who touched my clothes?'

That is the story. And in order to appreciate to the full the point I am about to put to you I would ask you to say to yourself, *aloud*, those last few words: '*knowing in himself that virtue had gone out of him turned and said Who touched my clothes?*' You have said them aloud? Thank you. One more request. Would you just remember, for a moment, the Apocryphal miracle, about Jesus as a child, striking another child dead because he collided with him? Thank you. I am sorry to make you work so hard, but we are both after the same thing, and if we can believe in one miracle, we can believe in all.

We are now ready to comment on this story.

And this is what we are forced to observe. The story was written fifteen hundred years before Paracelsus laid the foundations of modern medicine. It was written sixteen hundred years before Harvey discovered the true circulation of the blood. Nearly eighteen hundred years after it was written Fritz Antoine Mesmer was expelled from the most enlightened capital of Europe for suggesting that there was a strange healing 'fluid' which, in certain circumstances, flowed from one human being to another. And nineteen hundred years afterwards, a medium was put on a pair of scales in Paris, and weighed during a trance, in order that it might be proved (as it was) that during this state she lost, in 'ectoplasm', as much as fourteen pounds in weight.

And yet, all these fragments of petty knowledge are implicit in the simple story of this woman. 'Some virtue' went out of Jesus. He felt it, physically, in his bones and in his blood. It was quite different from the jostling of the crowd on all sides. It was some tremendous attraction, drawing 'virtue' out of his body, through his clothes, into another body. To-day we would be inclined to grant that in a very minor degree and in very special circumstances, similar phenomena may be possible. But in those days, any such theories would have been regarded as simply crazy. It would have been utterly beyond the powers of the most brilliant sages, philosophers and doctors to *invent* such a story. It would have been as easy for them as to invent a complete description of a Zeppelin. And yet, the man who, according to the doubters, 'invented' it, was not a sage nor a philosopher nor a doctor, but a fisherman — a man who, in general knowledge, would have been completely floored by a modern slum-child of six years old.

IX

We are beginning to feel desperate.

We are gentlemen of disbelief, but at the same time we would like to get out of this argument. Unfortunately there is only one exit, and over that exit is written in large letters FAITH. But we can't have faith. It's . . . it's silly, it's 'not done'. It's unscientific.

In despair we turn to the higher critics. Can't they do anything for us? Can't they switch the limelight on to some part of the story which proves it, beyond a shadow of a doubt, to be false?

The answer, unfortunately, is no. For the higher critics are really in just as uncomfortable a position as we are. As every year goes by they are being made to look more ridiculous. Why, even when they push their noses into the *Old* Testament, which you would have thought a good deal more vulnerable than the New, they have to draw them out again with a sharp cry of disgust, and all the libraries echo with their sneezing.

149

This may be irrelevant, but I can't help quoting here, with a certain malevolent delight, the discomfiture of that pillar of superior wisdom, the Rev. Samuel Holmes. The Reverend Samuel was an important contributor to *Peake's Commentary on the Bible*. He knew all about Joshua, at least, he thought he did. Elevating his nose in the air, and taking an antiseptic pen between his fingers he wrote, 'If this reconstruction of the history of the Conquest is approximately true, the narratives of one book are simply an unscientific endeavour to account for certain historical facts known to the writers. The last twelve chapters of the book are generally admitted to have little if any historical value. According to critical investigation the book appears to be a medley of contradictory narratives, most of which are unhistorical.'

After which acidities it may be safely presumed that poor Joshua retired behind his beard, in dudgeon. (I like the word 'dudgeon', which always makes me think of rather tough fish.)

The reader must excuse these flippancies, because I am feeling light-hearted. Not through any personal perversity but because Joshua, after all, is not in such a deep hole as the higher critics have endeavoured to throw him. And strangely enough the people who got him out of the hole are the people who dig holes, not with their pens, but with their spades, the archaeologists.

Professor John Garstang was for seven years director of the British School of Archaeology in Jerusalem. He was also director of the Department of Antiquities in Palestine. He was constantly on the spot near all the historical sites over which so much higher critical scorn has been poured. The historical sites of Joshua and Judges. Jericho, Ai, and Hazor. He says:

'I was deeply impressed with a sense of material reality underlying the historical narrative of Joshua and Judges. No radical flaw was found at all in any of the topography and archaeology of these documents.'

Professor Garstang (with his despised spade) also ended 'the difficulties of chronology which have long perplexed students. I found that not only were these records founded upon fact, but they must have been derived from earlier writings, almost contemporary with the events described, so detailed and reliable was the information.'

And yet the Reverend Higher Critic Samuel Holmes calmly stated, *before* these excavations, that most of the chapters were written eight hundred years later than Joshua!

'Irrelevant,' sniffs the Rationalist.

'I beg your pardon. It is not at all irrelevant.'

'We were talking about miracles.'

'Quite. But we were also talking about the higher criticism, a subject which *you* introduced. And this example of higher criticism is typical. Higher criticism gets higher and higher, but it always explodes in the end.'

'Not over the *New* Testament.'

'On the contrary. The higher critics have far worse luck with the New Testament than with the Old. I chose the Old Testament because I wanted to be scrupulously fair, and because it is far more vulnerable. And in spite of that, it is being vindicated more and more clearly every day.'

And indeed, this is literally true.

The spade confounds the pen. The man of action throws mud in the face of the man of letters. And all the ink of learning runs dry in the sands where the secrets of the Bible are hidden. They are magic sands. For many years the wind blows over them, while the scholar writes. And then, there is a storm, and in the morning, on the sands, something is shining. It is a text, glistening, golden, as fresh as on the day the prophet minted it. And the poor scholar has to rub the dust from his eyes, go back to his study, and start all over again.

x

'Science! Science! To our rescue!'

So might we gasp, in our last despairing efforts to preserve our dignity, as gentlemen of disbelief.

But Science, alas, can no longer hasten to the aid of those who stone the prophets. She herself is too enmeshed in the snares of a magic she does not understand. It is all round her, flickering from a thousand test tubes, dazzling her, bewildering her, filling her hair with sparks and her veins with a strange fire.

Science is dancing dizzily towards — what?

Well, wherever she may be dancing, she is not dancing away from the idea of a miraculous interpretation of life.

And whatever she is proving, she is proving one immense and eternally irrefutable fact, which is that man knows Nothing, without the help of Something. The man of Faith calls that Something — God.

Is the man of Faith a fool? Of course he is a fool.

Aren't we all? But he is not such a fool as the man of doubt, because he knows his own folly.

Every scholar wears a clown's cap. That is what Science is proving. Through the rhythm of the most learned discourses we hear the echo of the Jester's bells. That is what Science is proving. And every Q.E.D. ends in Q.U.I.

XI

Miracles.

They don't happen.

Very well. It is A.D. 1936. Before you is a black box. You paid ten guineas for it. You open it and turn a knob. And suddenly the room is filled with a woman's voice. You don't like the voice. You turn off the wireless.

Silence.

Silence, you say? Silence? *Why, the music is still going on!*

No, it isn't. We've turned off the machine.

What has that got to do with it? *The music is still going on.*

We need not continue the argument, which is indeed childishly obvious. And yet, I think that most of us are inclined to forget, when we turn on the wireless, that it is *not* the machine which causes the music. The machine is merely an ear — an intermediary. Of itself the machine is incapable of uttering a single squeak. It is a dumb, silent structure of wood and metal. It can only echo what it hears.

We forget this. We feel, in a way, that the wireless is

153

like a gramophone — that it is doing something of its own accord. It is doing nothing of its own accord. It is merely repeating a lesson.

This, when you really grasp it, is an awful thought. For this silence — this blankness, emptiness, which surrounds us in our quiet room, is a tempest of melody. The air is drenched with music, dizzy with song. The ether is a wild medley of voices, laughing, crying, sobbing, entreating. *Is*, I said. Not 'would be, if we turned on the wireless'. It *is*, whether we turn on the wireless or not. Schubert is in the room, and Mozart, and Beethoven, and the song of the nightingale, and all the music of this earth. And voices pleading, and voices angry, and voices that whisper, and are sad. And we sit there, wrapped in silence.

XII

Now let us see, for a moment, where we have arrived.

We inhabit a world which is unique in space.

The maker of that world, whom we call God, is presumably kindly disposed to us. (I dealt with that point in Chapter I and will say a few more words about it in a moment.)

Man has only just arrived on this world (in comparison with the immense ages in which the world was being prepared for him). And if God were to speak to him, instead of leaving him in a bewildering silence, God would choose to speak at about the time in which the Christian says He did speak.

In order to emphasize his words it is fairly obvious

that He would accompany them by certain signs of a very remarkable nature.

And that brought us to the miracles.

Now what did we find about these miracles?

Firstly, we found that the men who ask us to believe them did not conspire together.

Secondly, that the miracles are not vague but extremely explicit, and are told of many men, some of them important, who could have contradicted them, but did not do so.

Thirdly, that the men who told them had every reason for *not* telling them, for keeping silent about them, since their only reward for speaking was persecution.

Fourthly, that the miracles are totally unlike anything that has occurred in the world before or since. We proved this by referring to the miracles of the Apocrypha, which were invented.

Fifthly, that if the miracles were forged, the men who forged them were not only great literary artists but were animated by the purest and most God-like thoughts, since almost every miracle is a pendant to a moral. Christ heals. Men marvel and gather round. Christ speaks. That is the almost invariable procedure.

Sixthly, that instead of the miracles increasing with time, as we should assume they would do, if their source was Fiction and not Fact, the *first* gospel tells of more miracles than any of the other gospels, and that these miracles have *not* been added to. Which leads to the assumption that even if men *tried* to invent a Christian miracle, they could not.

And that, by the way, is rather an interesting little thought. I do not believe the greatest imaginative genius of to-day could forge a single story, about Christ, which would not sound hollow beside the immensity of his words.

Seventhly, that unlike every other God made by man Christ sometimes *failed* to work miracles, which sounds as if the men who were writing about him were writing *history*. And it also fits in with the legend that God came to earth as a man, with human failings.

Eighthly, that there are certain miracles, such as that of the woman with the issue of blood, which gives an account of a psycho-therapeutic event which could not conceivably have been understood by the man who wrote it. We decided, and rightly, that the discovery of these words in these ancient documents was as remarkable as would be the discovery of a detailed description of a modern aeroplane.

Ninthly, and somewhat irrelevantly, we paused to observe that the Higher Critics, who are the chief enemies of belief in the miracles, are being continually confounded — that the vogue of a Higher Critic is rather less protracted than that of a film star, and considerably less useful.

Tenthly, and still more irrelevantly, we turned on the wireless, just in order to show what clods we are. We *thought* we had ears. We haven't. The proof of that is that you, who are reading this, are sitting in the middle of a tempest of melody and discord. And you can't hear it.

I want to add an eleventhly, and then I want to say a lot of things which are very mixed up in my head, and will probably look rather foolish on paper. Still, here goes.

XIII

The 'eleventhly' is really quite simple, but you may not ever have noticed it.

It arises from the little synopsis to which I have so frequently referred you — the unique world, the voice of God speaking.

Have you ever realized one very strange and almost terrifying thing about Christ's words?

Have you ever noticed that he speaks — *like* God?

All the other little prophets *apologized* to the Almighty. Rent their garments, sought advice. All the other little gods were only too aware of their failings. But Christ, whom even the sceptics admit to be a perfect character, had none of this humility. It never seems to have occurred to him. He spoke as one having illimitable authority. He spoke, in fact, as God would speak.

Listen.

Here is Elijah. A great prophet of the Old Testament. He is staying in the widow's house. Her son falls sick, is on the point of death.

'And he said unto her, Give me thy son. And he took him out of her bosom and carried him up into a loft, where he abode, and laid him upon his own bed. And he cried unto the Lord, and said, O Lord my God, hast thou also brought evil upon the widow with whom I sojourn, by slaying her son? And he stretched himself upon the child three times, and cried unto the Lord, and said, O Lord my God, I pray thee, let this child's soul come into him again. And the Lord heard the voice of Elijah.'

157

And now, compare the action of Christ in similar circumstances. The story, by the way, is told us by Luke, who was a physician. It is also told in considerable detail. The date, the circumstances, the dramatis personae, and the name of the city, Nain, are all given.

'Now when he came nigh to the gate of the city, behold, there was a dead man carried out, the only son of his mother, and she was a widow; and much people of the city was with her. And when the Lord saw her, he had compassion on her, and said unto her, Weep not. And he came and touched the bier; and they that bare him stood still. And he said, Young man, I say unto thee, Arise. And he that was dead sat up, and began to speak. And there came a fear on all, and they glorified God, saying, That a great prophet is risen up among us; and, That God hath visited his people.'

'*Young man, I say unto thee, Arise.*'

The words are unique. No prophet before or since has equalled that assurance. If Luke was inventing that story he was inventing something utterly without precedent. He was also inventing something against his own interest. He was also inventing with incredible rashness, in view of the fact that he mentioned names and dates within the living memory of the persons concerned.

XIV

We come, then, to this.

The miracles of the New Testament are completely and eternally inexplicable to us as gentlemen of disbelief.

If they are fakes, nothing fits in. No theory is applicable. We suggest an explanation, and in the next breath we have to contradict it. None of the tangled mysteries of history offers a fraction of the difficulties in which those miracles abound.

On the other hand . . .

If they are genuine, everything fits in. History falls into its place. Hitherto inexplicable actions become as clear as daylight. Meaningless discourses become highly significant. And a dark cloud of lies resolves, quite suddenly, into a single shining truth.

This is a *fact*. It is not an opinion, or a vague assertion, but a fact.

We have therefore arrived at the position of an atheist who is doing a crossword puzzle, in which one of the words is GOD. If he will only write down that word the uprights and the horizontals fall into place automatically. Everything fits in. The puzzle is solved. The prize is won. But unfortunately, he is an atheist, and there is no such word in his vocabulary. And therefore he has to cross out the 'precious metal' in four letters, beginning with G, which ought to be 'gold', and the interjection in two letters which is obviously 'Oh' and the 'evil spirit' in five letters which is obviously 'Devil', and sit there twiddling his thumbs, because he will not admit that the 'Ruling Spirit of the Universe', in three letters, beginning with G, is GOD. If it were in four letters he might make it GOAT, which would fit in most admirably with his philosophy. But unfortunately it's only in three. A damnable Trinity, tripping him up.

X V

And now, it seems, we are in very sight of the treasure but our limbs are paralysed. Our brains, those foolish little grey jellies which are always giving us mental indigestion, are holding us back.

This is an absurd situation. For, all through the treasure hunt, we have been following the direction of those brains. We have said, 'All right, *you* take charge'. And the grey jellies have directed us, automatically, to the treasure.

But then, the grey jellies stiffened. 'There is something here which we do not understand' they seem to say. 'This is all highly irregular . . . monstrous. We admit that there appears to be a treasure over there. We can't find any flaws in it, even under the strongest microscope. But we *know* that there isn't such a thing.'

We have come to the most critical moment in this book, and perhaps in our lives. For it is now that we have to make the supreme test of forgetting our brains and following our spirits.

It is very like jumping off a cliff. Here, under our feet is the solid land. Behind us are the things we know and cherish, the kindly lights of a village street at dusk, trees with their sturdy roots thrust under the green fields, a cool river flowing, the echo of music and men's voices. Before us, space, and a voice. We are told that somewhere in that space is happiness, waiting for *us*, and an eternal strength, stored up for *us*, and peace.

We sway there, on the cliff. The little grey jellies

that are our brains shiver with apprehension, crying 'No, No. You will dash yourself to destruction. You will lose everything'.

The Voice says, 'Lo, I am with you alway, even unto the end of the world'.

'Madness, madness,' scream the little grey jellies. 'You are flesh and blood . . . nothing else . . . you are a decaying husk of matter, go back, go back to the street and make the best of your little hour.'

The Voice says, 'Be still, and know that I am God'.

We press our hands to our ears. We shut our eyes. The conflict of the two voices is tearing us, rending our spirits. We aren't strong enough for such torments. We want help. We cry out for succour. And we cry, to God.

And so, it comes. That is the miracle, the ultimate miracle for which we have been seeking.

It is so tremendous that it is indescribable. It is so triumphant that at first the Rationalist, who for years has been tortured by the sense of his own importance, may not quite realize what has happened. He is like a man in a quarry where a great piece of rock has suddenly been blasted away. He is nearly blinded and deafened by the explosion. But gradually, as he opens his eyes, he sees a fair landscape that stretches before him, and as he takes his hands from his ears, he can hear the birds singing.

I am unworthy to write of this mystical experience. I only ask you to believe that it is true.

When we have pulled ourselves together, I will try to be more practical, and suggest a very few simple directions that you may follow as you stand on this cliff of doubt — a silly sentence, but I don't feel able to search my grey jelly of a brain for the right phrase, just now. I feel too happy. I want you to share that happiness with me.

How funny this all is! We started this chapter with a microscope, and it seems to be ending in music. We began by treating miracles as 'phenomena' (and it is worth while to note that a 'phenomenon' is only a piece of grit which the little grey jelly cannot absorb) and we end by treating them as our birthright. For now, you and I are aware that every moment of this strange and lovely life, from dawn to dusk, is a miracle. Somewhere, always, a rose is opening its petals to the dawn. Somewhere, always, a flower is fading in the dusk. The incense that rises with the sun and the scents that die in the dark are all gathered up, sooner or later, into the solitary fragrance that is God. Faintly, elusively, that fragrance lingers over all of us. Sometimes we may not sense it. In noisy streets, in clamorous cities, the dust of the modern world may assail us, till we are breathless, panting for the sweet airs that drift from the little hill where once he cried, 'My God, my God, why hast thou forsaken me?' But always, there is that strange haunting perfume — the savour of true virtue — that is like violets in a twilit lane, and music, when soft voices die.

PART II

CHAPTER I

CRUSADERS OF 1936

I

I STOOD staring out of the window, feeling very miserable.

'It was madness to come here,' I said to myself. 'Complete madness.'

I continued to stare. The window looked out on to the wide lawns of Lady Margaret Hall, the women's college at Oxford which, for the moment, was the headquarters of that remarkable religious movement known as the Oxford Group.

It was about six o'clock in the evening, that exquisite moment when the sunlight, no longer pure gold, is tinged with silver dust. Over the lawns drifted an astonishing collection of people. Smart young women, shabby young women, bishops, soldiers, sailors. Smart young men, shabby young men, Cockneys, scouts, Indians, Chinese. Children. Very old ladies. Boys in shorts, kilts, flannels. Girls in tennis dresses. The sort of crowd one had never seen before. They had nothing in common, except that they all looked happy.

'Madness,' I repeated to myself, from my lonely window, 'madness, to come here. I *can't* plunge into that crowd.'

And I began to review with regret the strange chain of circumstances which had led me to Oxford.

I forgot who asked me to go. For some months

various correspondents had suggested that the movement would interest me, but I had disagreed because I didn't really know what the Oxford Group was.

'A sort of religious revival run by an American called Buchman, isn't it? Don't a lot of undergraduates get together and tell each other about their souls? I don't think it's my cup of tea . . . and anyway, I don't like public religious confessions. It's too like spiritual mixed bathing.'

That was what I wrote to one man who had asked me to go. But he refused to let me get away with it.

'The words "religious revival" are quite inadequate to express what the Oxford Group is doing,' he wrote. 'The word "Oxford" is utterly inadequate to describe its scope. And the phrase "house-party" is equally inadequate to describe its method of procedure.'

That letter intrigued me. And so, in a wild moment, I said I would go. I wrote to the Group, and received an invitation, by return of post. It all seemed very business-like. There were several pamphlets and circulars giving particulars of meetings, accommodation, etc. From one of these pamphlets I learned that my board and lodging would come to about 10s. 6d. a day.

10s. 6d. a day.

An unpleasant little thought came into my mind. 10s. 6d. a day was a good deal less than one would pay at an hotel, but surely there were many people who would find it beyond their means. Were such people barred? If not, who paid for them? And how did they get to Oxford? And how did they get leave from their work?

Was the Group only for the well-to-do? If not, who financed it?

These are the sort of questions which must inevitably occur to any man who thinks that faith, though an admirable quality, will not buy railway tickets nor pay hotel bills.

The extraordinary answer, which I found out soon after I arrived at Oxford, was that faith did precisely these things. There were down-and-outs from the Embankment, unemployed miners from Wales, quantities of poor young men and women from European countries. True, they were not all staying at hotels. Many were in great camps round the district. Nor had they all travelled by car, nor by first class steamers. They had come by lorries, by excursions, even by cattle-boats. 'But even *that*,' you may say, 'costs money. Where did they get it?' I don't know. All I know is that they got it. And they got it by faith. It never seems for one moment to occur to any members of the Group that there are such things as transport difficulties, nor that a minor problem like a job nor an impending operation, nor family troubles nor anything like that could possibly deter them from going at once to any part of the world where they felt 'guided' to go.

'Grossly impractical,' says the Rationalist.

Of course, it is grossly impractical. The only drawback, for the Rationalist, is that it happens, in practice, to work.

However, this is anticipating. We had better return to that first hour, where I stood looking out of the window on to the crowded lawn, feeling very lonely, and wishing that I was miles away.

11

I looked round the room. It was like hundreds of others in women's colleges — bright but very simple. There was an armchair. A screen railed off a primitive wash-stand. There were a few books on the little shelf on the mantel-piece.

On the mantelpiece lay a Group pamphlet. I picked it up. The first sentence was pretty challenging. It informed me that the first principles of the Group were 'absolute honesty, absolute purity, absolute unselfishness and absolute love'.

Somehow that appealed to something in me. The part of me, I suppose, which likes hard work. I have always detested skimping things — if I weed a bed, I weed it, and don't just pull off the tops of a few dock leaves, and if I learn a language I stick at the irregular verbs until I know them. The members of the Group were doing a tremendous job of work — they were trying to relieve mankind of sin, and they were going to the roots of the problem, with a vengeance, in that sentence.

I decided, just for fun, to accept the challenge, to see how it worked in the present situation. And as soon as I accepted it, I had a series of shocks.

I would like you to regard the little section which follows as a sort of indoor game. A truth game, which you play by yourself, in a quiet room. You may think that it will lead you nowhere. You will be wrong. You may think you are really rather a charming person, with perhaps a few weaknesses, but nothing to worry about.

You will be wrong. You may think you are already honest with yourself. You will be wrong.

Absolute honesty.

Well, how did it work at this moment? Why, for instance, was I sorry I had come? Firstly, because of purely material things. The room was a pleasant little room, really, but there was no private bath, and immediately I began on that track, I realized the quite ludicrous extent to which I was dependent on luxury. It made me see that my simple life was actually absurdly complex. Here I was, supposed to be a Christian, and I was worrying about beds, clothes, and wallpapers. It was so despicable that for a moment I thought it would be better to stop there. There was enough honesty for one afternoon, I felt. But I went on.

Absolute honesty.

Why was I afraid to mingle in the crowd outside? 'Because I might be asked a lot of tiresome questions about my books, and grabbed, and told to make a speech.' That is what I had said to myself as I stood in the window. But as soon as I tried this little game of absolute honesty, I saw that this was not the reason at all. The reason was exactly the opposite. I was afraid that I should *not* be grabbed, and that nobody *would* ask me to make a speech. To be quite honest, I had not the smallest desire to make a speech, but I had to confess that it was very nice to be asked.

Do you remember the story of Tennyson and Meredith? Tennyson was complaining bitterly about the number of people who spied on him, tried to catch a glimpse of him in his garden, hung about his front door.

'Spies, spies ... damn the whole lot of them!' barked Tennyson.

'You'd damn them much more loudly if they *didn't* spy,' observed Meredith.

Tennyson was very angry. But he would have been all the better for a little more absolute honesty like that.

'Go on,' I said to myself. 'Absolute honesty. What is the reason for this absurd self-consciousness, this feeling of being a new boy at school?' And I found that one of the reasons was an egotism that amounted to mania. And in case you feel very superior as you read this, ask yourself if you have never been shy, too. If you admit that you have, then you must admit to an inflated egotism. Shyness is only self-importance, turned upside down.

I went on and on. After half an hour of absolute honesty I felt vain, cowardly, and actually unclean. In other words, I had realized the consciousness of sin. It is a strange feeling, and an extremely salutary one. For the little pamphlet told me to confess my sins and to ask forgiveness. I did so. I went down feeling that I had just had a mental bath.

I walked across the lawn. These people were now my friends. I went up to a young man who was walking about alone, with his hands in his pockets.

'I've just been trying out absolute honesty for the first time,' I said. 'It's pretty disturbing, isn't it?'

'You haven't learnt the half of it yet,' he laughed. 'You wait till to-night.'

He took my arm, and we strolled towards the river. It seemed as though we had been friends for years.

And I began to realize that whatever else you might say about the Oxford Group, there was an atmosphere about them that was, to say the least of it, electric.

III

Miracles happened that night. But before I can tell of them, I would ask you to pause for a moment's retrospection.

I wish to emphasize the fact that this is not a book about the Oxford Group, nor has it really been inspired by the Group, except in certain of its later passages.

I must make this point quite clear, because there are probably many things in the book with which the Group would disagree.

This book is simply the record of one man's spiritual progress from darkness to light, and in this connection it may be interesting to point out that, in a certain sense, I have been writing it all my life.

It began fifteen years ago, in a little school story called *Prelude*, which I wrote when I was at Marlborough. In this book there is a chapter called 'Stale Incense'. This chapter is largely autobiographical. It describes the reactions of a sensitive boy to the horrors of public school 'religion'. This is how the chapter ends:

'After chapel he went slowly to the wood, and sat down by the bathing-pool. By and by he drew from his pocket the little crucifix. He dropped it rather wistfully into the water and watched it dive with a little flash of silver into the deep black weeds below. He wondered if that was, in a way, symbolical of what Christ had done, a flash of light, darkness again, and a crystal bubble breaking on the surface of the waters. He stretched out his hand as though to drag it out, for he felt dimly as though he had lost a friend.'

You would say that a man who had no 'religion' in him, who had finally finished with Christ, would drop the subject. But that was impossible. One was haunted, persecuted (at least that was how it seemed). Always the Hound of Heaven pursued, while I found myself feverishly proclaiming my disbelief in the most unlikely places, as though to reassure myself.

There was a slight collection of impressions which I called *Twenty-Five*. The book was not unsuccessful, and helped to create a vogue which was followed by so many other young men that I wished I had never written it. But there was something lacking in the books which followed *Twenty Five*. The 'something' was an appalling sense of futility, a tragic emptiness behind the light-hearted prose. In case you think I am reading into that book (which is not very important and was somewhat carelessly written), a significance which is not there, I may perhaps be forgiven for quoting a few lines from the last chapter:

'And thus, abruptly, I end. A line drawn, a cigarette thrown out of an open window, a pile of manuscript pushed into the corner of one's desk, waiting to be sent to the typist.

'And thus, I suppose, youth ends. A line drawn under

one's eyes, a sudden realization, as one is laughing or drinking, that the "stuff which will not endure" has worn itself threadbare. To what purpose? God alone knows. Not I. . . .

'We, this post-war generation, have formulated a creed of which the first principle is that happiness does not exist. We are only young as long as we can cheat ourselves, as long as we can go on dressing the future in bright garments, and spinning a web of illusion over the past. . . .

'Accept the joke of life for what it is worth. It is not such a very brilliant one after all. . . .'

That was nine years ago.

This sense of utter futility may be seen at its culminating point in an essay which I published two years later on Mr. Hilaire Belloc. When we have quoted it, these extracts from the works of Beverley Nichols will cease.

The essay on Belloc ends with a regret that he was an orthodox Christian:

'As I bade farewell to that black-coated figure, I was sorry for two people. I was sorry for him because I felt that he had nailed his colours to the wrong mast. And I was sorry for myself because I had no colours to nail to any mast at all, and the world seemed singularly grey.'

You see? It is all a variation on the little theme from *Prelude*, where the boy drops the crucifix into the water. 'He felt as though he had lost a friend.'

And so, though this book is not a record of the Oxford Group, it would be incomplete unless I paid my tribute to this amazing movement. For though I myself had found, by long and painful search, that Christ was indeed God, though at last I had come, by many winding, stony ways, to a shrine at which I could worship, it was not till I went to Oxford that I found, once again, the friend whom as a schoolboy I had rejected.

I V

And now for the miracles.

We dined in hall. About three hundred of us. It was a very simple dinner with nothing to drink except water. I sat opposite to Dr. Buchman and next to Canon Streeter, who has one of the best theological brains in Europe. We didn't talk about religion. We talked about Mussolini.

Canon Streeter was feeling very pessimistic about the Italian-Abyssinian dispute, and said that he thought that most of the papers were wrong in suggesting that a settlement would be found within the framework of the League of Nations. From there we went on to talk about dictators in general.

It was then that I had my first glimpse of the revolutionary principles of the Group.

I was saying something rather obvious about the difficulty of getting any idea 'across' in certain countries of Europe. 'Take the question of religion,' I said. 'After all, in these days a handful of unscrupulous men backed by machine-guns can force almost any doctrine on to a whole people. They can compel them to believe any creed which may be convenient. They are so incredibly powerful . . .'

And then a young man, who had not previously spoken, leaned across the table, smiled, and said very quietly:

'They aren't more powerful than God.'

'I beg your pardon?'

I had heard what he said, quite plainly, but the remark was so unlike the sort of thing one was accustomed to hear at dinner parties that it caught me unawares.

'They aren't more powerful than God,' he repeated. And then added, in the same breath, 'Do you mind passing the toast?'

I did not at all mind passing the toast. In fact, I was extremely glad to have the opportunity of passing any-thing at all, if only to give me a breathing space.

Another young man, who was not in the group, asked 'Are you going to try to "change"[1] X——?' (I use the symbol X—— to conceal the identity of a certain dictator whose name is not very *bien vu* in this country.)

'Why not?'

'You're not serious?' said the sceptical young man.

'Why not?'

'Well really, wouldn't you be taking on rather more than you could manage?'

'Rather more than God could manage, I suppose you mean?' said this remarkable young man, with unper-turbed calm. And then, he said 'Do you mind passing the water?'

I felt slightly dizzy. These people talked of God as if He were a reality. He was as much a part of their lives

---

[1] I should explain that when the Group has made a man surrender his life to God they describe him as 'changed'.

as food and drink. He was all-powerful, and so no request they could make of Him could be too fantastic.

I realized that here, in a world of doubt and despair, was something of limitless faith and hope. In a world of negatives here was a supreme positive. Life seemed to be beginning all over again.

v

An hour later. The lecture hall. It was packed with people, most of them young. There were about three hundred people in this hall, and there were about a dozen similar meetings going on all over Oxford.

I have seen in my time a number of 'religious revivals'. The least attractive was run by the 'hot-gospeller' Aimee Semple McPherson in Los Angeles. Her ambition was, apparently, to turn Christ into a vaudeville artist, and she succeeded extremely well. However, I have described in another book[1] the distaste which this compound of hysteria and vulgarity aroused in me.

But here, the word 'revival' did not seem to apply. There was no hysteria. No vulgarity. No snobbery. No sort of sensationalism. There was only a tremendous sense of power and peace and happiness.

Let us try to be as objective as possible. If I tell you that these people had surrendered their lives completely to God, you might merely yawn and turn the page. But if I tell you that a woman who had been a hopeless drug

[1] *The Star Spangled Manner.*

addict, who had spent years of her life screaming in
nursing homes, who couldn't wear evening dress because
her arms were so covered with morphia piqures — if I
told you that she had come to a meeting of the Oxford
Group, with morphia in her bag, had left the meeting and
chucked the stuff in the river, and had never taken nor
desired any since, then you may sit up and take interest.

That was one of the first confessions I heard.

'But *how* did she do it?' you may ask. 'It's one of the
most difficult things in the world, to give up drugs.'

'By surrendering her life to God,' is the answer. Which
is enough to make most people cluck their tongues against
their teeth with impatience. But it happens to be true.

Let us continue to be objective. We can only judge this
thing by results.

Look on the platform. A shabby little man with one
of the strongest Cockney accents you ever heard is speaking. He is telling about his life, with a charming racy
humour. Two rooms in a tenement. Five children. Unemployed. Illness. Most of the money used to go on
drink. 'We were muck and we knew it . . . muck, the
wife and I and the kids.'

He met the Group. There are still the two rooms in
the same tenement. Still five children. He is still unemployed. There is still illness. But now they are sons of
God. He ends up by a plea to those who have not yet
been 'changed':

'You could be as 'appy as we are, if you want.'

Again, I point out, we are dealing with *results*. I am
not asking you to pass judgment on the methods, which
you can call black magic or blue magic or any sort of

magic you like. I am only asking you to believe the facts.

One after the other they got up, and told the same story. There was a brilliant Cambridge mathematician. One little detail in his confession might amuse you.

'Before I met the Group,' he said, 'I was in a regular mess with my advanced pupils. When I was working out an intricate problem on the blackboard, I sometimes used to get stuck. When that happened, I'd wave my hand airily to the class and say, "You can finish that for yourselves". Then I used to retire behind the blackboard. But now, I say quite frankly "Sorry, but I'm stuck". As a result, we're all friends, we've got a new interest in our work and they trust me as they've never trusted me before.'

But these are puerile little faith cures, you may say. Perhaps. Though I do not think it is so puerile to rescue a woman from the power of drugs, nor to bring a smile to the face of a down-and-out, nor even to make a Cambridge professor admit he's been wrong. However, if you are after stronger stuff, listen to this.

I had not been at the meeting for an hour before I saw, rising to his feet, a young man whom we will call Y. I can't give his real name, because the whole point of this story is that Y was, without exception, the most immoral man I have ever known. He was so actively vicious that one said, 'Really, I mean . . . Y is extremely amusing and grand company, but one can't possibly be seen about with him.'

When I had last met him, about three years ago, his marriage had been on the point of breaking up. He was in danger of losing his post because he was never entirely sober. In addition, I suspected that he had begun to take drugs. He had many of the signs which indicate the cocaine addict, the significant slovenliness of details of the toilet, the blue-rimmed eyes, the little twitch of the nostrils. No, one really could not know Y.

As for Mrs. Y, she was nearly as bad. She was aggressively and offensively anti-religious. She had not many decent friends, but those she had she offended by the vulgar blasphemy of her conversation. There were two children. Neither had been baptized, neither had heard the name of God. They were fortunately very little things, who had been kept awake on too many nights by the sound of wild parties. And when the parties were over there were usually loud-voiced recriminations between husband and wife.

Well, three years ago, they had come to Oxford for a new and last sensation. As they motored up Y said:

'I think I'm beginning to get cirrhosis of the liver.'

'Thank God,' replied Mrs. Y, 'you deserve it.'

'Thank what did you say?'

'God. That's who's running this show, isn't it?'

She spoke with her usual contempt. She was looking forward to a certain amount of malicious amusement. There were people here who believe in God! A loving God, too, if you please! She'd stop that, soon enough — she'd wake them out of their damned complacency.

They went for one night, hating life, hating each other, believing in nothing.

They stayed for a week. When they went away they were lovers again. They were believers. And life was supremely great and exciting.

I have pieced this story together partly from what Y told me afterwards and partly from what he said at the meeting. I shall never forget staring at him, as he stood there, facing the crowd. He spoke very quietly and simply and the old humour flickered through his sentences. And afterwards, his wife followed. She was terribly pretty, and charmingly dressed. She did not look at all like a religious 'maniac'. She looked extremely sophisticated. Only, unlike most sophisticated women she had a light in her eyes of complete and radiant happiness.

If you have read so far you will agree that all this is either deadly dull and quite meaningless or highly exciting and intensely significant.

It is either one or the other. And it is only dull and meaningless if it is untrue.

You may call the people deluded. You may say that they *didn't* get help from God. You may call it religious hysteria, anything you like. Very well. Call it so. It makes no difference. For the one thing you can't deny is the result — namely, that two utterly miserable and worthless people, in a state bordering on physical collapse, hating each other and only able to bear life by constant recourse to drink and drugs, were suddenly and apparently permanently transformed into happy lovers, of true value to the community, with an abundant faith and hope.

Those are facts. They are quite indisputable *facts*.

It is also a fact that such transformations are not worked by medicines, nor kind friends, nor considerate relatives who die at the right moment and leave one £5,000 a year.

The people who have been cured, very definitely cured

180

of very definite physical and moral diseases, say that they were cured by surrendering their lives to God.

Couldn't we try to believe them, just for a moment? To stop treating the thing as a wild sort of joke and to treat it seriously?

No, we couldn't, you say? You want more evidence. Very well. Here it is.

V I

It is the following morning. Sunday morning.

The scene is a cinema. The largest cinema in Oxford.

For half a mile around, the roads are blocked with a dense stream of traffic. Motors, lorries, bicycles, and thousands of pedestrians.

You would think that Garbo and Chaplin and Gary Cooper and all the rest of them were appearing in person, judging from the eagerness with which everybody is pushing forward. But these people are not interested in the stars, at least, not in those stars. They have come, quite simply, to worship Christ. And they have come from all over the world to do so.

Those of you who have been occasionally depressed by our empty London churches on Sunday mornings would have been intensely stimulated by this sight. In London, in most of the big cities, the pulse of worship throbs feebly. It throbs principally among old ladies, who may be seen (God bless them) alighting timidly from their cars in the great squares, and vanishing through the porch, to sit in twos and threes while a weary vicar drones

comforting words to them and a full-throated and somewhat irresponsible choir sings anthems, and covers up
the thin quavering of a few tired voices.

'A few more years, and these tired, gentle old ladies
will be dead, and then ... who will remember Christ?'
That was what I used to think, before going to Oxford.
I had visions of our churches in decay, closed, or turned
to secular purposes. One saw the Church as the last
refuge of a few dying eccentrics.

But now . . .

I stood in the great hall of the cinema, watching the
crowds throng past. I was genuinely excited. I turned to
my companion.

'This is news,' I said to him. 'News with a capital N.
Genuine front-page stuff. Are all the newspapers crazy?
Why don't they do something about it?'

He looked at me and smiled. 'Why don't *you*?'

'I ... well ... ' Then I laughed. There is something
so positive about these young men that you can't deny
them. 'All right,' I said. 'I'll do something.'

I seem to be doing it, now.

But please, stand with me, in that hall, and recapture
some of the thrill of it. All around are great glazed pictures of the stars. Joan Crawford with her goggle eyes.
Adolf Menjou with his synthetic smile. Dietrich with
the eyebrows like butterfly's antennae and the disturbing
mouth. Gary Cooper making the most of his masculinity.

And all these exalted ones are being passed by. Completely ignored. Nobody troubles to look at them. Joan
Crawford goggles and goggles and not a glance does she
get from any of the troops of eager young men who are

passing in. Menjou leers away for all he is worth. Nobody cares. Dietrich's eyebrows seem to go higher and higher in astonishment, and her mouth, no longer disturbing, seems to be disturbed. 'Are there *no* fans in this crazy crew?' she seems to be saying. And Gary Cooper is just a piece of paper, glazed and painted, a piece of paper that will one day flutter on the hoardings in a cold wind, and find its way to the dust heap.

I repeat, that is *news*.

It is more than news. It is — well, it is a sort of revelation. As you stand there, facing the posters, and the crowds, it seems that the smiles on the posters are like the grins of skulls, as though the paint had peeled away, revealing nothing but futility and decay. But the smiles on the faces of this advancing army of Christians are different smiles, that will not fade, and are warmed with an eternal glow. Which is a most embarrassing observation, you may observe. And if sincerity is embarrassing, and a positive belief in God, and a heart that is not set on the things of this world — if these things make you feel shy, then you would have felt very shy indeed at that meeting. You would have felt naked, and not a little ashamed.

VII

The meeting is just beginning. We go to our seats in the Press gallery. We can only just squeeze in. We look down at the immense crowd. We feel that we have to pinch ourselves to make sure that we are not dreaming.

'These people are here to worship God,' we have constantly to remind ourselves. 'They are not here to see a star. Nor to hear a witty speech. Nor to get anything material. They are here because they have discovered that the man who loses his life shall find it, that the man who gives shall receive, and that the only happiness, yes, *happiness*, is to be found by rigid adherence to the four principles of 'Absolute honesty, absolute purity, absolute unselfishness and absolute love'.

We continue to stare down at the crowd.

'It is 1935' we have to say to ourselves. 'These people aren't all mad. Nor uncouth. Nor dribbling at the mouth. They bear none of the marks of the eccentric person who dabbles in odd movements which are inspired by purely earthly motives. They don't look like the dress-reformers, for example. Dress-reformers always look as though they had been to a fancy-dress ball the night before, and had dropped their latch-key out of their togas, so that they couldn't get back to change before breakfast. Nor do they look like members of pacifist societies, who always make me feel that there is something to be said for militarism after all. Nor like any of the people who go in for 'isms'. They look — well, they look as if they had their feet on the ground and their heads in the sky. And that, I believe, is how God wants men and women to be.'

However, we promised to be objective.

The meeting is being led by a little Scotsman who was once secretary of the Young Communist Party of Great Britain. He played a considerable part in the General Strike. He was one of the sharpest thorns in the flesh of capitalism. Now, his whole life is devoted to the service of Christ through the Oxford Group. He has been 'changed'.

Next to him on the platform is a big employer of labour. I had seen him arrive at the meeting in a very resplendent motor car. He calls the little Scotsman by his Christian name.

No. The ex-communist is not a 'blackleg'. He has not been tempted by a cushy job. He hasn't *got* a job, in the sense of regular, salaried employment, because in the Group there are no such things as salaries, nor hours of labour. You merely do what you can, and you take no thought for the morrow.

The words of the little Scotsman ring out: 'This is the one way in which we can bring a truer dignity to labour. This is the greatest revolutionary factor, when the Holy Spirit becomes active in the lives not only of the employers but of the employees. *Our movement will cut across all artificial barriers, and will revolutionize all our ideas of economics in relation to supply and demand.'*

Is it not possible that we may call this a miracle? Those of you who have lived among communists, as I have lived, in the Glasgow slums, who have realized the intense, vitriolic bitterness of their outlook, who have gauged the depths of their fanaticism may be inclined to agree that it is.

And that reminds me of something which should really come later, but may be inserted now, because it is so apposite. I frequently asked members of the Group what was their attitude towards economic problems. Did they attack capitalism? Were they socialists? What did they think, for example, of the theory of Social Credit?

This theory is often quoted, not without reason, as an example of Christianity in economics. How did it strike them?

Their answer was nearly always the same. 'We're not interested in economics, as such. We believe that almost *any* economic system will work, if the men who work it are filled with the spirit of Christ. We also believe that almost *any* economic system will fail if the men who work it reject Christ. That is why we do not attack Capitalism. There is nothing in Capitalism to attack — you might as well "attack" the multiplication table. The abuses of Capitalism are not to be found in the system, but in the hearts of men. It is the *men* you must change, not the system.'

If you quarrel with that argument you can only do so on the grounds that it sets too lofty an ideal. And those are the only grounds on which you can quarrel with *any* of the lessons of Christ.

Let me be objective again. I wish you could have been there, in that immense crowd. I can describe certain aspects of it, but I can't even indicate the most extraordinary aspect, the *simplicity* of it all. For instance, if I tell you that a mill girl from Lancashire came forward and confessed, you will probably visualize somebody leaping on in clogs, waving her shawl, and doing a 'number'. Instead of which, a quiet, rather pretty little creature, very plainly dressed, stepped up, and without a trace either of embarrassment or of 'showing off', just told us all of the happiness she had gained '... Sum of t'girls said I was soft, balmy ...' she said. 'They realized we'd *all* been balmy, before we were changed.'

Oh — if I only had you sitting before me, making your little interjections, raising your little eyebrows, and murmuring polite superficialities about all this! I'd answer you, all right! I'd answer you by telling you that 'happiness' is a word that *means* something — that it is the thing for which gold is paid, and health broken, and hearts too, for which endless endeavour is made. And that these simple people (though some of them weren't always so simple, either) have found it, for ever, by giving their lives to God, and receiving them back again, changed and glorified.

VIII

I ought to write the word 'objective' on my desk, and keep it there, because I know you are principally interested in the living 'exhibits' of this miraculous meeting.

Well, searching my memory at random, I recall a half-caste woman. 'I was a missionary's lapse,' she said. You can giggle at that sentence if you please. Or you can see in it something strange and terrible. It depends on who you are. But I don't think you can giggle at this. 'I feel proud to-day,' she said, 'proud. White women have spoken to me as though I were a friend. As though I were just a woman, as though they didn't see the colour of my skin. No white woman has ever spoken to me like that before, except a woman who was blind, and didn't know. But to-day, I feel proud.'

Half-castes, communists, mill-girls! 'A queer crew,' you may exclaim. Well, I have emphasized the democratic side of the Oxford Group in order to counteract the silly legend that it is a snobbish movement. If you wish for a more 'respectable' element we can switch to the President of the Vancouver Stock Exchange, a dignified, grey-haired figure, standing very erect. He follows the Lancashire mill-girl. He makes a highly technical speech about international currencies. He traces the volatile movements of the franc, exposes the artificial respiration which is being administered to the mark, spins a dollar coin between his fingers and finds that it doesn't ring quite so true as we had imagined, and even stares sterling out of face. And as he talks, we gradually realize that these currencies are beginning to look a little cheap. They are like a child's counters, blown by the winds of destiny. They have no more intrinsic value (and by 'intrinsic' I really mean 'eternal') than those little circles of green and scarlet with which we once played tiddley-winks on the nursery floor.

He pauses. And then, in the same tone he would use if he were seconding a motion to approve the re-election of a board of directors, after a successful company meeting, he says, 'I know, and you know, that in the modern economic world there is no such thing as worldly "security". It does not exist. There is only one security which the sane business man can recommend. And that is, the guidance of God.'

Is *that* 'objective' enough for you? You don't become President of a Stock Exchange merely for being a good boy and knowing your texts, do you? Nor do you hold that position, for any length of time, entirely by your knowledge of the Old and New Testaments. You hold it because you've got a good brain. Which makes me think that there is one thing the President omitted to say, namely, that the test of a 'good brain' can only be measured by the standards of Christ.

I could go on and on. I could show you down-and-outs from the most depressed areas of Wales, smart young undergraduates, middle-aged women, artists from Chelsea. But it would only be repeating what you already know, and if you are not impressed by that, you will not be impressed by anything. You see, it is the sceptic whom I am trying to convince, trying to catch the echo of the sort of question he might ask. Here, I think, is one of them:

'This is all very well,' he might suggest, 'and the movement appears to be of undoubted value to a number of individuals. But I fail to see how you can claim for it any national importance. As for its being a real international force, well, if you'll forgive me for saying so, that's just a lot of bunk.'

We will answer this question with three brief examples.

Firstly, Canada. At this meeting a message is read out from the Prime Minister of Canada to the effect that *Canada is easier to govern since the visits of the Oxford Group.* Yes, I know, it sounds fantastic. But if you knew the details, you would realize what the Prime Minister meant. You would be able to tell stories of prisons in which men undergoing long sentences of solitary confinement had been transformed from sullen animals into happy, peaceful, sane individuals. You would be able to quote more than one prison in which 'house-parties' had been arranged *within the prison walls.* You would know of whole factories which had been 'changed', and run on the principle of 'absolute honesty, absolute purity, absolute unselfishness and absolute love'. And you would have heard of thousands of families, all over the country, which had been turned from hostile, warring centres of discord into loving units of a single great community.

Secondly, South Africa. At the meeting, a young colonial quotes a passage from a newspaper stating that 'since the visit of the Oxford Group the race problem has been considerably alleviated'. When I first heard that, I naturally considered that he must have got hold of some stray gossip paragraph from an unimportant and frivolous newspaper. On the contrary, I discovered later that this was the sober opinion of a large section of the most conservative press. And those who remember the story of the little half-caste woman who was 'proud', because white women had spoken to her as if she were a human being and not a piece of trash, the thing does not seem quite so impossible after all.

Thirdly, the Scandinavian countries. From here comes the most remarkable evidence of all. For some years the Group has been concentrating on Norway and Denmark, because it is rightly felt that these countries form strategic points from which the conquest of the rest of Europe may be directed. The results already obtained in these little countries will sound almost incredible to the man who looks upon international affairs from the material point of view.

One example will suffice. Ever since the first visit of the Group the governments of the Scandinavian countries have been constantly in receipt of mysterious envelopes marked 'Oxford' and addressed to the Treasury. *On opening these envelopes the astonished officials have discovered, reposing in them, cheques to the amount of many thousands of pounds in payment of income tax which had been fraudulently withheld.*

Cheques, you may note, not paper money.

These examples could be multiplied to the point of weariness. They could be reinforced by examples of the changed attitude, in these northern countries, to all the most vital problems which beset a country, the problems of war, of finance, of national health. However I think we may now assume that the sceptic who considers that this movement is of slight importance has a rather harder case to prove than he imagined.

I X

There is nothing 'new' about the Oxford Group. There is nothing 'sectarian'. It contains thousands of Catholics, Presbyterians, members of the Church of England, Quakers — there is hardly any form of Christianity which is not represented in it. It does not ask a man to change his religion. It *does* ask a man to allow his religion to change *him*.

But though there is nothing new, there are two principles in the movement which are vital. They are both derived, purely and directly, from the teaching of Christ.

The first principle is that of confession, which implies a consciousness of sin. (If you are a Rationalist, please don't be bored by this, nor indulge in snortings and growlings. It happens to be rather interesting.)

Consider this little trifle of sin. My old argument against a 'consciousness of sin' was that I had been given certain instincts at birth, for which I had not asked, and for which I was not responsible. Since these instincts had been kindly implanted in me by the Creator, I had followed them. It was ridiculous to blame me for following them. God made me as I am, and if I wasn't perfect, it was His fault, not mine.

This seemed a fool-proof argument. Actually, of course it is the most grotesquely silly argument ever invented. Carried to its logical conclusion, it means that if I murder my grandmother, throw my baby brother into the bath, torture animals, forge cheques and live on an exclusive diet of heroin, I shall still be 'without sin'. If you deny all responsibility for yourself in small matters, and if you allow the instincts which were given you at birth to be the sole criterion of your behaviour, then you must also deny all responsibility for yourself in large matters. And not only for yourself but for your neighbour. And if your neighbour happens to have an 'instinct' to hit you on the head with a croquet mallet and to run away with your wife, you must not for one moment suggest that he has sinned. You must, on the other hand, congratulate him warmly for the magnificent example he is giving of a courageous surrender to his instincts.

This question of a 'consciousness of sin' is, of course, a fundamental principle of Christianity, and it can only be gained through Christ. To which the Rationalist may reply 'That's an odd argument! It's like saying "although you feel perfectly well, I know a marvellous doctor who will invariably prove to you that you are ill".' Well, I suppose it *is* like saying that, except that the Rationalist has omitted to add that the doctor charges nothing and invariably cures the patient. However, we have really come too far in our treasure hunt to pay quite so much attention to the Rationalist. We will assume that we are addressing somebody who is, at least in theory, a Christian, in order to emphasize the importance of the Group's attitude to confession and the consciousness of sin.

They have a practice they call 'sharing', which means that they confess to one another and not only to God. A lot of cheap laughs have been gained at the expense of the Group through a misunderstanding of this practice.

'I regard it as pernicious,' said a very bright young vicar to me, after I had come down from Oxford. 'It might lead to very great abuses.'

'Have you ever tried it?'

'Certainly not.'

'Why not? Because it's so unpleasant?'

He began to grow red in the face. 'Are you suggesting that I shirk confessing my sins in prayer?'

'No. But will you give me a quite honest answer to a question?'

'Yes,' he said rashly.

'Very well. And when you've answered it, I'd be glad if you'd tell me, equally honestly, whether it was easier to tell the truth to me, to a man, face to face, or whether it would have been easier to shut your eyes and mumble a few polite phrases to God?'

'You are extremely offensive,' said the vicar.

'Not nearly so offensive as I'm going to be.'

I then asked the question.

I did not get an answer. But by the horror in that man's eyes, I knew the answer he would have given, if he had dared.

X

It is difficult for one who is conscious of sin to hold any very intelligent communication with one who has not that consciousness. It is like speaking to a man with a wart on his nose who persistently denies the existence of that wart. But it is very certain that until this consciousness is born there is no possibility of spiritual growth. And as long as there is no possibility of spiritual growth, you will continue to be obsessed by fears of every description.

The members of the Group believe in sharing because they realize man's infinite powers of self-deception. Let me give you one example of this, and then we can go on to the second great principle of the Group.

A friend of mine who had made a considerable name for himself in the world of letters came to a house-party, was very interested, stayed for a week instead of a day, made friends with another writer, and experimented in 'sharing'. This is what happened.

He began by saying, quite honestly, that the only thing with which he reproached himself was the fact that he was inclined to drink too much. 'But then,' he added, 'I really only drink to help me in my work. I get so damned tired nowadays that I have to have a couple of glasses of sherry in the morning, or my pen won't work, and between four and seven I have to have two or three strong whiskies.'

That was how he began. Then, he suddenly flushed. *Why* did he have to work so hard, to flog a tired brain with artificial stimulants? Well, to make money. But he *had* plenty of money. Yes, but not enough saved to bring him in an independent income. But *why* this haste to get an independent income? And then it gradually came out. He was being blackmailed. Had he done what the black-mailer suggested? No, not exactly. Well, in a way, he supposed he had. He finally admitted that he was completely guilty.

What happened then? Well, then he asked for 'guid-ance'. Guidance is the second great principle of the Oxford Group members. They believe that those who are in tune with God receive explicit and detailed instructions with regard to the conduct of their daily lives, if they ask for it. They may not know what to ask for, they merely ask for guidance, and they get it. I believe that there are certain somewhat acidulated bishops who strenuously object to this idea. If they do, I fail to see how they reconcile their objections with the teachings of the Bible . . . a book which, apparently, certain bishops have not yet found it necessary to read. For example, Christ said 'And all things, whatsoever ye shall ask in prayer, believing, ye shall receive'. And St. Paul, in unequivocal language, made it very clear that those who did not know what to ask for would receive 'guidance'. St. Paul said: 'Likewise the Spirit also helpeth our infirmities: for we know not what we should pray for as we ought: but the

Spirit itself maketh intercession for us with groanings which cannot be uttered.'

And so our friend asked for guidance. He was told beforehand that he would receive a message which would be completely simple, sternly practical, and quite unexpected.

This was exactly the sort of message which he received. He was told to go and 'change' the blackmailer.

At which, no doubt, there will be loud and prolonged laughter, digs in the ribs, and girlish shrieks. I have never been averse to adding to the gaiety of nations — consciously or unconsciously — and so I hope that the laughter will go on for a long time, till your ribs ache. And I will continue to stand on the platform with an idiotic expression on my face, and only very occasionally tapping the desk with my finger-nails. But when the laughter dies down — for laughter, like all lovely things, is transient, and leaves no trace in the empty spaces where once it rang — I shall bring the story to a close by observing that this is exactly what my friend did.

Feeling crazy and light-headed, and wondering if he were walking into some horrible trap, he set off, one afternoon, through mean streets, knocked at a certain door, and confronted a certain man. The man was surprised to see him. It was usually *he* who had done the calling. This was indeed an unexpected honour. Perhaps his victim had come with an idea of making a final settlement. That's what blackmailers always want — final and permanent settlements, which are renewed, finally and permanently, every six months.

Well, a final and permanent settlement was made. Not

in cash. Nor in any of the things of this world. But in a common faith in a man who once died to save — black-mailers.

Perhaps this story should have been headed 'Believe it or Not'. I hope you will believe it. It is true. And I would ask you, for a very brief space, to recall its develop- ment. It began with a man confessing that he drank too much. Why? To help his work. Why? Because he was afraid. Why? Because he was being blackmailed. Why? Because he had sinned. You see, he came, at last, to the 'consciousness of sin'. And as soon as he came to that consciousness, as soon as he confessed, he asked for guidance, and he got it. And life, instead of being a haunted, fearsome thing became suddenly sunlit and wonderful and fearless.

For the benefit of the agreeable Rationalist, who is always peeping over my shoulder, I will add a tail-piece:

Moral. When being blackmailed, don't consult your solicitor. Get in touch with the Oxford Group.

Their address, by the way, is Oxford Group, Brown's Hotel, Dover Street, London, W.1.

x

Guidance.
That is the second principle of these gay young crusaders.

It is a beautiful word. It suggests a controlling force, personified in a good shepherd, who is pleading, night and day, to lead the world to the only true peace and happiness.

But people react very oddly to words. Some people don't want to be guided. They are so proud of their little eccentricities (which are usually to be explained in terms of glandular secretions), so devoted to their own personalities (which are merely a compound of chemicals and salts, handed to them in a penny packet at birth) that they wish to 'do it all themselves'. To them, there is something faintly humiliating in the idea of 'guidance'. It is as though an expert in Baroque architecture were being constantly jogged on the elbow by a tiresome little guide at San Souci. 'I know as much as you do,' he feels inclined to say, 'and if we are being frank, a damned sight more.'

All right. My object in writing this book is different from the object I have had in writing my other books. All I want is to get as many people as possible to share with me in the excitement of living Christianity. And if the word 'guidance' offends you, let us pluck it out. Let us call it 'magic'. That's a grand word, too. A great many Rationalists believe in magic. They believe that rabbits really can be made to jump out of top hats. The only question they never ask is 'Who made the rabbit?'

However, we must elbow aside our little Rationalist friend. All we desire is that he should pay attention, for a moment, to this question of guidance, and in order that he may do so with a clear conscience, we will let him call it 'magic'.

I want to give a very personal example of guidance.

After the meeting in the cinema, and after many walks on enchanted lawns, and many conversations with people who seemed to have the gift of a happiness that was not of this world, I felt an urgent, insistent desire to seek for guidance myself.

'They say you have only to ask,' I said to myself. 'I will ask.'

The light was fading as I walked back to the hotel to which I had moved. It was the longest day of the year, or nearly the longest. About ten o'clock. The hotel was not particularly romantic, and my room was singularly devoid of charm. Still, I was in search of 'guidance'.

The wallpaper was on the squalid side, and the tap in the hand-basin kept on dripping. I tried to shut the window because there was an irritating noise of bicycle bells, but the sash was broken, and the window stuck. So I sat down in the chair a little grumpily, and stared at the paper in my hand.

It was a little pamphlet called

THE QUIET TIME.

Underneath was a line from the Psalms — 'Be still, and know that I am God'. There was a sub-title — 'A few outline notes on the guidance of the Holy Spirit in the life of the individual through attentive prayer'.

The pamphlet began by saying that 'Experience shows that the individual is guided by God, in the following ways . . .'

Before I could read further, a whole chorus of noises assailed me. The clocks of Oxford began to strike. While they were striking, the bicycle bells redoubled their frenzy. A chambermaid, outside in the corridor, began to rattle keys in locks. A party of noisy Americans, arriving at the front porch in a large car, became very vocal about the treatment of their luggage.

'This is ridiculous,' I said to myself. 'Prayer is only really possible for the rich, or for people who live in cathedral cities. One wants lofty pillars, with pale fingers of light creeping slowly down them. One wants a distant organ, and not the sound of bicycle bells. How on earth are the poor to pray, with children shrieking in the tenement yard, and the noise of a dozen radios?'

Then I thought of the little hunch-backed man on the dole who had spoken at the meeting the night before. He had five children. They lived in two rooms. They always began the day with 'A Quiet Time'. He looked radiantly happy and peaceful.

And the thought of him made me feel a little cheap. I tried again. I read on. I came to the 'conditions for an effective quiet time', with its requirements of 'absolute trust and obedience to the Will of God, and the carrying of it out immediately, as it is revealed by the Holy Spirit'.

The pamphlet here told me to look up two passages in the Bible, and to read them before going on. One was from the Book of Proverbs, the other from St. John. I looked them up. Here they are:

> O ye simple, understand wisdom: and, ye fools, be ye of an understanding heart.
> Hear; for I will speak of excellent things; and the opening of my lips shall be right things.
>
> Proverbs viii, 5-6

That was at once a challenge, and a promise. Was it an empty challenge, and a false promise? I should soon know.

But these words, somehow, seemed to bring drama into the room. I turned to the other reference:

Howbeit when he, the Spirit of truth, is come, he will guide you unto all truth; for he shall not speak of himself, but whatsoever he shall hear, that shall he speak; and he will shew you things to come.

St. John xvi, 13

'He will shew you things to come.' Yes, that was dramatic too. The noises in the street outside, and in the hotel itself, seemed to be fading away.

I read on. There were simple little questions to ask oneself. I asked them. There were simple little prayers to make. I made them. From time to time, I turned to the brief texts which were indicated. And every text was a fresh draught of comfort and peace. The feeling of drama remained, but all sense of urgency had gone. How else could one feel when, very quietly, in an empty room, one had spoken, with the Psalmist, those words which are as gentle as a caress . . .

Rest in the Lord, and wait patiently for him: fret not thyself because of him who prospereth in his way, nor because of the man who bringeth wicked devices to pass.

Perhaps it was getting late. The noises outside seemed all to have stopped. I don't believe I thought of looking at my watch. All I remember is that it seemed as though invisible hands had closed the windows and shut out all sound, as though the place around me were hung with curtains of peace.

And then, I came to the crucial moment, the moment when my friend had told me that 'guidance' would come.

Very slowly, and with the greatest concentration, I read:

'In the attitude of "Speak Lord for Thy Servant heareth", wait patiently and quietly, listening for what He has to say, what He has to reveal to us concerning ourselves, what piece of work He wants us to do.'

I laid down the pamphlet. I closed my eyes, and waited.

And then, suddenly, as though it were flashed in luminous letters across a screen, I saw a very simple sentence, of the utmost significance to me.

It was so simple but so significant, that automatically I sprang to my feet. I shall never forget that moment — standing up in the funny little hotel bedroom, breathing rather quickly, completely astonished.

'It works . . . it *works*!' I kept on saying to myself. I couldn't grasp it. At last I knew what to do. 'It works!'

X I

'What works?'

I beg your pardon. I had forgotten that a number of Rationalists were in the audience. But the sharp tone in which he asks the question is enough to remind me. And the Rationalist, according to his lights, would be quite justified in speaking not only sharply but sarcastically.

'*What* works? What was the sentence of such significance? Did you get the winner for the Derby? Or an idea for a new novel? Or what?'

It was something rather more remarkable than that.

Before I tell you what it was, may I remind you that

my friend had told me that if I put myself, even for a
few minutes, in God's hands, if I made a complete surrender, I should receive very definite, practical and
immediate 'guidance'. He had said:

'I haven't the vaguest idea what it will be. It will
probably be something quite unexpected. It usually is.
It will certainly be something of the utmost simplicity.
It always is. The one thing which is certain about it is
that it will be immensely valuable, *and that you could
not possibly have got it with human aid.*'

My 'guidance' was a classic example of this.

It was completely unexpected (I wasn't thinking of the
problem when I began 'the quiet time'). It was of the
utmost simplicity. It was immensely valuable. I could not
have got it by human aid.

It was concerned with a very intricate legal problem.

For over a year a friend of mine had been involved
in a law-suit. He had engaged the most eminent counsel.
He was being served by a firm of solicitors of the highest
ability and integrity. Every aspect of the case had been
discussed at length. Skill, learning and money had done
all they could do.

I was one of the principal witnesses and I was miserable about it. I had a horror of law-courts, and for
months I had suffered nightmares in which I had
found myself in the witness-box under a hideous fire of
cross-examination in which every little folly and weakness
of my past life would later be blazoned forth in head-lines
to the evening newspapers. I cannot say more, because,
at the time I write, the case is still unsettled. All that I
may say, without impropriety, is that although my fears

were unreasonable (to the best of my knowledge, un-reasonable and foolish), they were nevertheless acute and absorbing. I could not get rid of them. The whole of life was in a shadow.

Nobody could help me out of that shadow. Nobody had any suggestions to make. 'You'll just have to trust to luck' was all they said.

In a single sentence, in that 'Quiet Time', a complete, final, and staringly simple solution was given to me.

I wish I could tell you what it was. All I can say is that I knew that I had, *at once*, to telephone to a certain person, and to tell that person certain things. It was a difficult, unpleasant, humiliating thing to do. But I did it.

I hung up the receiver, and stayed quite still, in the little telephone box. I remember that it smelt rather strongly of scented cigarettes.

'That's over,' I said to myself.

I felt I ought to go and have a double brandy, to celebrate. Somehow, I didn't want one.

'That's over,' I said again.

The learned counsel, the brilliant solicitor, the eminent chartered accountants ... they had served us well. But ten minutes in a quiet room, asking for help from God, had served us better.

And, I must repeat, the case at the time of writing, is still unsettled.

I must also remind you that the author of these words is not particularly gullible, and was born with a constitutional tendency to look gift horses in the mouth. Nor is he a prey to superstition of any kind. In other words, I want to remind you that it is 1936, that I know it is 1936, and that I am not covered with dust and whiskers. And in spite of these facts, I assert that in room number 262 of an Oxford hotel in this year of grace, by trying the power of faith, I gained, from a penny pamphlet, in a dozen words, a solution to a problem which all the legal luminaries of England and all the love of friends could not solve.

It seems, to say the least of it, worth a penny.

XII

Nice young men who took firsts at Balliol, and are never able to forget it, are inclined to sneer at people who emphasize the *practical* results of following God's guidance.

'Really, I mean, *faintly* nauseating, don't you think? treating God as though He were a tipster?'

That seems to be their response to the news that a woman has been cured of drugs, through prayer, or that an unhappily married couple have found peace, by surrendering their lives to God.

'Really, I mean, a *shade* repulsive, isn't it, asking Christ what to do about the man next door?'

Anything is nauseating, and anything is repulsive, if you like to make it so. You can think loathsome things about a rose. You can think very beautiful things about the most horrible disease. A great many artists have painted pictures of roses which are as dreadful as pictures of diseases. I am among them. Rubens, on the other hand, found poetry and lasting loveliness in the shambles of a butcher's shop.

But such homilies do not affect the nice young man from Balliol. It is better to accuse him, straight away, of the one sin which he really abhors, the sin of muddled thinking.

When he expresses a quivering distaste for the man who asks God for something, and expects to get it, he is really expressing a distaste for the Christian who acts as a Christian. He is accusing the Christian of acting against the spirit of Christ because the Christian is doing exactly what Christ told him to do.

That, I must gently insist, as a Balliol man, is an accusation which is not in the best traditions of Balliol thought.

Christ said — 'And all things, whatsoever ye shall ask in prayer, believing, ye shall receive'.

Either that means something, or it doesn't.

If it means something, it means that what you ask from Christ, believing, you receive.

Isn't it worth trying ... just for once?

CHAPTER II

CHRIST AND SEX

I

WE have now reached a point where we can say, with complete honesty, that Christ has become a reality to us. It may be that he will become the greatest reality of all, the Reality of Realities. We are not sure. But we *are* sure that the pious figure has come to life, that the painted image has stepped down from its niche. For us, the words of Christ have no longer a parsonic echo, nor are they any longer a mere lilt of lovely Elizabethan prose. They are living words, and the voice which utters them is quiet but tremendous, strangely personal, and yet as wide as the winds.

It is therefore fairly obvious that we should begin to listen to this voice to hear if it has anything to say about our personal problems, and it is equally obvious that for most men the first and most urgent series of personal problems which need consideration can be grouped under the heading of Sex.

(The reader who may open the book at this page is asked to believe that we are dealing with very practical realities when we talk about 'listening to a voice'. To use a homely parallel, it is really as simple as turning on the wireless, if you will only try it. However, to believe that, you will have to read the chapters that have gone before, and also the chapters that are to come.)

The reason why the average man will begin by submitting his sexual problems to Christ is because sex is, of course, the most powerful of all man's instincts except the instinct of hunger. You cannot escape from it. It throbs with your heart and beats time with your brain. It guides your feet on strange errands through strange streets. It sings in your throat and glistens in your eyes and shines in your hair. You *are* sex. And thus, it is vitally important that you should know yourself, because on that knowledge your whole life depends. For sex can be used in two ways. It can be used as a bright sword, with which to cut through the undergrowth of life. Or it can be used as a chain, which clanks after you in a gloomy rhythm to your passage through the world.

The Rationalist may observe 'But an Eastern prophet, who lived nineteen hundred years ago, cannot possibly have anything to say of any value to the generation of 1936. Christ only preached a sort of poetic celibacy. . . .'

Did he? It is a pity that the Rationalist does not read the New Testament.

Christ was more modern than any 'modern' in his attitude to sex, for the simple reason that he was outside the little clock-face limits of time. However that is anticipating. Before I can discuss this matter of sex I shall have to give some indications of my credentials for doing so, or, if we may coin a word, my 'discredentials'.

II

It may be observed that the persons who are most emphatic in their assertions that they have been saved, by religion, from the snares of sexual extravagances, are frequently those whose knowledge of such vices is extremely limited. I have listened to a number of evangelists who, from their own account, have been sunk deep in the mire of sin, and always I was reluctantly forced to the conclusion that they were flattering themselves. Those words are bitter and they were meant to be bitter, because there is nothing more revolting than the pride of the sinner in the depths of his sin, there is nothing more distasteful than the exultation with which certain religious vulgarians point to the depths of the valley from which they have emerged in order to emphasize the height of the peaks to which they have attained.

We need not endeavour to emulate these persons. It is enough to state, as a matter of documentary interest, that we are in as good a position as most people to note that the world, since the war, has been considerably more licentious than even the average evangelist is inclined to realize. And as I wrote those words, a number of pictures came to my mind. The streets of Berlin, before the Nazi regime, when every body was for sale, when hunger drove boys and girls to submit themselves to revolting humiliations, when the wildest whim of the most exotic taste could be gratified for the payment of a few marks — one knew of those things. Harlem, in the boom days, a few hours before dawn, when white met black, and forgot colour in a universal darkness of lust, shot through with the chemical fires of bootleg gin — of this one was aware. Paris, when everybody was taking drugs, and when the bars were full of white-faced, gibbering young men and women, whose bodies were like broken fiddles, the nerves strung tighter and tighter until they snapped — one had 'friends' among these people. Every year, as I travelled about, I noticed the increase in the numbers of the pathetic fraternity in 'guides'. There were some capitals in which every other man seemed to be a 'guide'. They were funny little men, mostly, with wizened faces. I expect they probably kept large respectable families in the city's suburbs.

That was organized vice. Any dreary man with no morals and enough money to make a Cook's tour of the world will be able to tell you smoking-room stories about that sort of thing till you feel sick. It is rather the disorganized sexual irregularity which concerns us here. And I do not think it is an exaggeration to say that a large number of respectable parents in England and America would swoon with horror if they knew a quarter of the sexual life of their children in this year of grace. They would shut their sons and daughters from home. This picture is, admittedly, farcical, if you think of it in terms of the slamming of quantities of virtuous frontdoors. But the facts, as I have stated them, are true. And the reason they are true is because the parents in question have failed, most criminally, to set before their children the picture of Christ. *They* had it set before them in their young days, the distant days before the war. It was so beautiful a picture, so glowing, so stainless, that a little of its radiance haunts them yet. But in countless homes, the repercussions of war blew the picture off the wall, and the parents forgot what it looked like. They were too harassed, too disorganized by a thousand urgent problems.

.The time has come to hang the picture, once more, on the wall. To see if we can learn any message from the eternal eyes. And if our parents will not do it for us, let us do it ourselves. For we are young, and eager, and tortured with desire.

We need not be afraid that we shall receive only a blank stare. Most assuredly we shall learn something, even if that something is unwelcome to us. Nor need we fear that we shall not be understood. For however clouded may be our eyes, however dim the light, we shall come to a gradual, almost awful realization as we gaze on his portrait. We shall realize that we are looking, no longer, at a figure in a stained glass window; we are looking at a man who moves and breathes. *A man who must have known and shared the earthly desires which we associate with the word 'sex'.*

Christ was God, in man incarnate. In everything that man rejoiced, he rejoiced, in everything that man suffered, he suffered. Sex can help to raise a man to heaven, or it can help to crucify him. To say that Christ was outside all this, untouched by it, is to make his life a sham.

III

Let us make this point so clear that if we are to diverge, after having come so far together, we shall each know which path we are guided to take.

We will not indulge in 'speculation'. We will seek no authority but that of the Bible.

One of the first things we learn about Christ, in the

Bible, is that he was tempted by the devil. 'If thou be the Son of God command this stone that it be made bread.' So spoke the devil to him in the arid wilderness, when he had been fasting for forty days. The fact that Christ rose above this, as above all other temptations, does not prove that he was *immune* from temptation. If he had not felt the pangs of hunger, there would have been no merit in the reply that was wrung from him. 'It is written that man shall not live by bread alone.' It would be merely an empty moralization which would have been blown away on the desert wind and been forgotten.

It was the same during the agony in the garden. Not only had he the ordinary man's capacity for feeling pain, but the ordinary man's capacity for dreading it. He knew only too well the horrors that were waiting him on the cross, and his body reacted accordingly. When he made that poignant supplication — 'Father, if thou be willing, remove this cup from me ...' we are told that, as he prayed, 'his sweat was as it were great drops of blood falling down to the ground'.

Christ, in fact, was *man*, complete, whole. He was not a god walking about in a framework of bones and flesh. He was man — the perfect fusion of God and man. And it is a monstrous emasculation of the Son of Man to suggest that Christ did not know and suffer the temptations of sex. If you regard this idea with disgust you had better go back to your painted image, which knows no emotions, which is gilded by a sunlight which it does not feel and tarnished with a rust of which it is not aware. But as you do so, you must honestly admit what you are saying about Jesus Christ. You are saying that he had every human emotion except the greatest human emotion of all. He was hungry, thirsty, yes, he was tired, angry, exalted, yes, but he was untouched by sexual desire. That is what you are saying. I simply do not believe it. And I cannot understand a man who *does* believe it gaining any comfort from prayer, in his sexual problems, to such a Christ, because all the time he is assuming that he is speaking to Christ of some emotion which Christ did not understand, and share, and conquer. And such an assumption is blasphemy.

Of course, Christ understood. Of course, he was tempted. Somewhere in the world must be the dust of some body which once he saw, and seeing, thought it beautiful. Desire must have entered into him, desire which, with a golden gesture, he transformed, lifting it from the corruptible to the eternal, from earth to heaven.

And that desire was the measure of his 'sin'. And the fact that he conquered it is the measure of his inspiration to all men for all time.

I V

This 'golden gesture' which Christ made towards sex is called, in these days, 'sublimation'. And our problem is to discover, with his help, to what extent the average man and woman can practise sublimation, and to what extent it is desirable to do so.

Sublimation is a fine word which, like many other fine words, has been given an ugly echo by the bastard 'science' of psycho-analysis. It should really imply a sort of mental elevation, a conscious transmutation of energy into higher channels. Psycho-analysis has given it a merely hysterical interpretation. The mind of the amateur psycho-analyst is full of lurid little paragraphs from Jung and Kraft-Ebbing concerning elderly governesses who have been removed to padded cells, shrieking texts from St. John, because they had not been afforded the dubious satisfaction of physical intercourse. The word 'sublimation' conjures up for him a ghostly cohort of pale priests with furtive eyes and fumbling fingers, of frenzied evangelists with high blood pressure and inflamed imaginations, of silly little undergraduates, with no girl friends, and a crucifix over their mantelpieces.

I know *now* that a man can clear up his 'complexes', eliminate his 'phobias', lay bare his 'repressions', and obtain a healthy mind far more effectively by spending five minutes on his knees, seeking the help of Christ, than by spending five years on a divan, seeking the help of a psycho-analyst. And when I say 'know', I mean 'know'. And if you will forgive me for saying so, I have just a little more background for my knowledge than a large number of young men and young women who think that Freud knew more about sex than Christ. Because, you see, in the old days, I was a Freudian too. There were very few of the works of Freud and Jung and Kraft-Ebbing and Pfister and all the rest of them that I had not endeavoured to digest. And while I was endeavouring to digest them, I saw all life in terms of sex. Every symbol was a phallic symbol, and every normal taste was a fetish. I could hardly see a woman looking into a boot-shop without silently accusing her of a morbid passion for high-heeled shoes. The manufacturers of mackintoshes, I felt, must all be in a wild state of sexual complexity. And as for a woman who wore ear-rings . . .

To the average healthy reader this will all sound like double-Dutch. It *is* double-Dutch, if you don't know the psycho-analysts. But there is a very clear interpretation of it, to which I will refer shortly.

In the meantime, I was psycho-analysed myself. It was in Budapest. A weird and nightmare experience. Snow was heaped high over the tragic city. The Danube was black under a sky of steel. Through streets that were almost deserted an impoverished population tried to carry on a parody of living. And there I lay, in an over-heated room, while a little man asked me fantastic questions about my youth. He charged £20 an hour.

The little man had a European reputation. But I, thank God, had a sense of humour. And also, I think, a sense of shame. And suddenly it struck me that this whole procedure was a mixture between a roaring farce and a particularly distasteful Grand Guignol thriller. The hot room, the searching questions, the intolerable egotism of it all — me, me, *me* — I was sick of myself. The city was outside, and the poor people, and the snow and the clear air — that was where I belonged. And that was where, with abrupt apologies, I went, and where, in spirit, I have remained.

v

Once again we have been side-tracked.

We had decided that Christ, being man, must have

known desire, and that he transformed it to glory by a 'golden gesture'.

To this transformation we affixed the modern term 'sublimation', and asked ourselves to what extent 'sublimation' of sex was possible or desirable for the modern man and woman.

Before we go to the highest authority, the authority of Christ, let us try to clear the ground, so that we shall know what we want to ask him.

Well, obviously, complete sublimation of sex for all men and women would mean that the world in a hundred years time would be empty, except for a few bewildered centenarians. And that is a prospect to which we need not give our attention.

Therefore a 'certain amount of sex' (an absurd phrase, but I can't find a better one) is not only permissible in the eyes of God, but essential.

The point is how much? And of what nature?

It is here, I am afraid, that I shall strike many of my readers as very unorthodox. All I can promise is that I will, in the end, test this unorthodoxy under the searchlight of Christ's scrutiny. If my words are false, in that light, we shall both realize it, soon enough.

Firstly, we must realize that the essential rights and wrongs of sex have absolutely no relation to the *law* of any particular country. Unless we divorce sex from any conception of man-made law we shall never have any clear ideas about it. It is true that in many respects a civilized country's legal code does, at least, pay lip-service to Christianity. As some eminent jurist, whose name I have forgotten, observed 'Christianity creeps into the statute book'. But in the matter of sex, Christianity and the law have been divorced, for the simple reason that the law does not realize what Christ's attitude to sex really was.

And the reason that the law does not realize this, is because the Christian official doctrine towards sex is based, not upon Christ, but upon St. Paul.

As soon as we wrote the word Paul, we put our finger on a whole host of sexual complexes and phobias (as the psycho-analyst might say), which Paul has incorporated in the Christian fabric, in the name of Christ, but against his spirit.

I say that with the utmost diffidence, for St. Paul was chosen by God as the instrument through which the message of Christ was to be propagated. To accuse Paul of misinterpreting the message might therefore be regarded as tantamount to accusing God of choosing a faulty instrument. I do not think such an accusation would be either very just or very relevant. We might as well accuse God of choosing twelve imperfect disciples! Whenever man has touched the message of Christ, man has endeavoured to mar it. And though Paul was a great man, a stupendous spiritual genius, he was not God, he was man. And it is to Paul that the Church has listened in the matter of sex, not to Christ.

These are hard words but they can be proved. For once in a way I find myself in agreement with Bernard Shaw, when he wrote 'There has really never been a more monstrous imposition perpetrated than the imposition of the limitations of Paul's soul upon the soul of Jesus'.

VI

'Unto the pure all things are pure.'

If Paul had said only that, he would have served his master truly. The phrase is not only a fragment of great poetry but a profound psychological observation and a quite practical guide to everyday conduct. Later on we shall revert to this phrase, but in the meantime we must see how it was confused in Paul's mind with a number of emotions which can only be called prejudices, which are no more inspired by Christ than by the man in the moon.

Why, only a few sentences before this lovely line (which comes in his Epistle to Titus), he was guilty of an intolerant generalization about a whole people. He is warning Titus against the Cretans. 'One of themselves,' he writes, 'even a prophet of their own said "The Cretans are always liars, evil beasts, slow bellies".'

'This witness is true,' he retorts. 'Wherefore rebuke them sharply.'

Liars — evil beasts — slow bellies! These, we are asked to believe, are the characteristics *of a whole people*! Can you imagine Christ, who always saw through the crowd to the individual, saying a thing like that? It is the sort of thing you expect to hear from a crusty old fogey in a Piccadilly club, when he is summing up the merits of the Germans or the Indians or the Russians, or other races whom he may deplore.

However, this has nothing to do with sex. I merely mentioned this little angry outburst, which is set side

by side with a beautiful fragment of philosophy, to show
how strangely were the elements mixed in Paul. Heaven
knows, he had reason to be angry. He himself had sacri-
ficed everything in life for Christ, and through his efforts
he transformed a Jewish sect into the Catholic church,
and created, from an obscure version of Judaism, the
outlines of Catholic theology. And it is for the very
reason that his achievements were so immense that we
must endeavour to understand the mind in which they
originated.

It seems to me impossible to avoid the conclusion that
it was a mind which had not conquered sex.

It seems to me equally impossible to avoid the conclusion that though, with Christ's help, Paul usually
managed to 'sublimate' sex, there were moments when he
went wildly astray from the spirit of Christ. And however far he strayed, the Church always followed him.

Which is the reason for a vast amount of suffering,
bigotry, obscurantism and hatred in the world to-day.

VII

Before you throw away this book in disgust, I want to
ask you a question.

Have you ever read the first epistle to the Corinthians? Yes? Then have you not noticed something very
strange about it — something almost uncanny? About
woman's hair? With every allowance for the fact that a
certain amount of rigidity of procedure was desirable,
since the early Church was in danger of losing itself in

swamps of hysteria, it is impossible for a modern reader to sympathize with Paul's constant storming against women who prayed to God without covering their heads.

'The sabbath was made for man, not man for the sabbath.' These were the quiet words of Christ, on a matter of tremendous importance.

What are the angry words of his apostle, on a petty detail? Here they are: '*If a woman be not covered, let her be shorn!*'

We rub our eyes. It is as though we were back in the Old Testament again. 'But if it be a shame for a woman to be shorn or shaven, let her be covered,' he adds.

It seems incredible. Even more incredible when we read on. Shaw, it seems, was certainly right when he called Paul the Eternal Enemy of Woman. Listen to this: 'For a man indeed ought *not* to cover his head, forasmuch as *he* is the image and glory of God. But the *woman* is the glory of the man. Neither was the man created for the woman, but the woman for the man.'

There is some mystery, here. We can't get over that feeling. The world, Paul thought, was about to end. At any moment the faithful might be caught up in glory to Christ and here he is, at this vital moment, wasting time on the subject of a woman's hair. It would not be so strange if, on other matters, he had been narrow-minded. But over and over again Paul had shown himself a master of compromise and common sense. His discourse on circumcision alone would prove that.

However, on this trivial matter, he is adamant. 'If the woman be not covered, let her be shorn!' And in a passage of extraordinary pleading he demands: 'Judge in yourselves, is it comely that a woman pray unto God uncovered? Doth not even nature itself teach you that if a *man* have long hair, it is a shame unto him? But if a *woman* have long hair it is a glory to her!'

VIII

These passages are from the Bible. Word for word. The exhortations of Christ's greatest protagonist.

What do you think of them? What do you think of this fuss about women's hair being covered?

Please do not evade the question. Does it strike you as Christ-like?

In order to help you to answer, just remember a few of the things that Christ saw and did. Christ said 'Take no thought for the body, what ye shall put on'. Christ talked, casually, with prostitutes in public places. To him they weren't prostitutes. They were just ordinary, unhappy people whom he could help. Christ sent the flame of his scorn over the Pharisees, a flame that flickers to this day in the searing words 'Ye make clean the outside of the cup and of the platter, but within are full of extortion and excess.'

Would Christ have told the women of the world that they could not plead to God unless they first put a hat on?

Well, would he?

You have to answer that question (which is 'blasphemous' only inasmuch as it is an accurate précis of St. Paul's doctrine), in order to realize how far the

Christian attitude towards sex has departed from Christ. For centuries women have been sitting in church with their hats on. Big hats, little hats, smart hats, shabby hats. They would feel naked and ashamed without them. If you asked them why, they would not be able to tell you. Certainly, the last thing they would say is that they were wearing their hats because, once, a wild and tortured prophet had seen a woman's hair and had found that it floated, like a devil's veil, between him and his vision of God.

Yet that, I believe, is the truth.

IX

I hope that I have given you a shock. It was my intention to do so.

The Christian teaching towards sex has largely dominated the world. And the Christian teaching towards sex is *not* the teaching of Christ, but the teaching of St. Paul.

And however much we may venerate St. Paul as a supreme servant of Christ, however humbly we admit that in many respects we are not fit to touch the hem of his garment, however thankfully we may read certain of his words which shine, like stars, guiding us to the gates of heaven, I think that we are blind fools to ignore that fact that St. Paul, though he was a prophet, was also a man, and that he was a man in a flaming temper against his own instincts.

There are many passages in the epistles which flatly

contradict the teaching of Christ. There are an equal number of passages which read like the denunciations of that strange and powerful character, the Reverend Davidson, in Somerset Maugham's famous story, *Rain*. Consider the epistle to Timothy, with its phrases about 'they which creep into houses and lead captive silly women laden with sins, led away with divers lusts'. The word 'creep' is so vivid that it suggests that the apostle, in imagination, was creeping into the very houses he condemned. The word 'silly' expresses an assumed contempt for something which, indeed, frightened him more than he dared to admit.

That is why he was so bitter against the women who added to their allurements by artificial means. He simply cannot bear that they should walk about the streets 'with braided hair, or gold, or pearls, or costly array'. No, no! Women must adorn themselves 'in modest apparel, with shamefacedness and sobriety'.

On those words, and not on Christ's superb charity to the Samaritan woman at the well, the Church has raised its strange and twisted edifice of sexual doctrine. On those words, and not on the gentle smile he gave to Mary of Magdala, generations of 'Christians' have based their authority for acts of intolerable oppression. On those words, and not on Christ's immortal challenge 'He that is without sin among you, let him first cast a stone at her . . .', laws have been made to shut out the light of the world, prisons have been built for the sole purpose of breaking men's hearts, and the Church itself has sent away countless thousands of decent people from its doors.

That is the penalty we have paid because we have

listened to the words of Paul rather than to the words of Christ. And once again I find myself in agreement with Shaw, whose words could hardly be bitterer. 'Paul was no more a Christian than Jesus was a Baptist: he does nothing that Jesus would have done, and says nothing that Jesus would have said, though much, like the famous ode to charity, which he would have admired.'

x

But here I part from Shaw with a loud and emphatic good-bye.

Before I explain why, let us sum up our progress to date.

We have observed, with wonder and veneration, the 'golden gesture' which Christ made towards sex, and have asked ourselves how far we can imitate that gesture ourselves.

We have decided that most of us cannot imitate it perfectly and that it is obviously against God's intention that we should do so.

We then asked how far we are supposed to 'sublimate' sex, and in order to arrive at a correct answer we decided that we must rigidly exclude from our minds any conception of man-made law.

We came to this decision because these laws are based, not on the teaching of Christ but on the teaching of Paul, who, in matters of sex, appears to be not only divergent from Christ but flatly in opposition to him.

And so where have we arrived?

It may perhaps help us to come to a decision if we see

224

what Shaw has to say about it. After all, Shaw has talked more common sense about sex than any man living. As a result of that common sense he came into violent collision with the Censor on many occasions, he was regarded as anti-Christ by a large section of the community, and, at times when he was the only man in the world who was standing squarely on his feet, was inevitably accused by the rest of mankind as standing on his head. He might, but did not, reply: 'Well, at least I have a head to stand on.'

However, when Shaw begins to talk about sex in relation to Christianity, every bull's eye he hits is an Irish bull's eye. And the reason is that no man, however brilliant, who has not been filled with the spirit of Christ (which is a spiritual and not a mental phenomenon) has really any authority to dogmatize about Christ. This will sound intolerable to the average free-thinker, but it is really true. No man who has not actually felt the indwelling presence of Christ, who has not claimed his promise 'I am with you always', who has not realized him with an overwhelming assurance that is infinitely more real than any earthly pleasure or pain, can know what Christ really meant about sex or about anything else.

'You are hitting below the belt,' Shaw may say. 'You are manufacturing a convenient mystical fog from which you can dogmatize, and you are telling me to shut up because *I* can't see through the mist and you say *you* can.'

I am not doing anything of the sort. A mystical experience does not dull a man's senses. It does not impair his intellect. If it did, the Jesuits, for example, would be at the mercy of any cheap demagogue, whereas their minds are subtler and more penetrating than those of any other body of men in the world.

'All right,' says Shaw. 'Fire away. What do you object to in my assertions?'

We will tell him. Remember, we are concerned to find out how far the average man ought to sublimate his sexual instincts, in other words, to what extent his body is keeping him from God. And as soon as we hear what Shaw has to say about it we feel as though there had been an explosion which definitely clears the air. For what he has to say is utterly intolerable. He says:

'Christ perceived that nobody could live the higher life unless money and sexual love were obtainable without sacrificing it.'

If Shaw, even for one second, had been filled with the spirit of Christ he would have seen that this is really an insult, not only to the God in whom he does not believe but to the dignity of the human spirit in which he does believe. At first sight, the remark has a sort of dreadful common sense. Man must first have leisure, man must first be purged of earthly passions, before he can seek God. That is what Shaw is suggesting. In practice it means that man must first have £1000 a year, in order to have a quiet mind and must also have a mistress before he can pray. That was, admittedly, a nauseating sentence to have to write. Shaw will agree that it was nauseating. The odd thing is that it was a logical deduction from Shaw's own remark. Yet, Shaw has one of the cleanest and most vigorous minds in the world. 'Which only shows you,' as one might say, how dark and tangled are the roots of sex.

Christ, of course, never suggested, as Shaw has suggested, that prayer can only flow from a body that has been purged of its sexual passions by another body. Christ never suggested, as Shaw observes, that an overdraft is a barrier that shuts man off from the Divine radiance. Christ was not concerned with overdrafts. He said, 'Take no thought for the morrow'. He was concerned only with man's approach to God. If the body weighed a man down to earth, then the body was accursed. But if not . . .

XI

This is a difficult and tangled subject. I know what I want to say, and I can say it to myself, in a quiet room. And I believe that then I speak the truth, and do not offend. But on paper, it is not so easy.

I am really asking a question: 'How far can a man or a woman, who is truly animated by the spirit of Christ, use his or her body as a means of pleasure?'

Thank God, we have got the question straight, at last.

And thank God, we have got the answer too. Of that we are completely certain. The answer is — 'Ask Christ'. It is an 'evangelical' answer, but that does not impair its truth, however 'sophisticated' you may think yourself. It is a complete and all-embracing answer.

And I believe that the man who *does* ask Christ this question will occasionally receive advice which a number of people would regard as shocking. I do not believe that the guidance he may receive will always be orthodox in the eyes of the world.

There is a deeply interesting passage in the Codex Bezae which might be quoted at this point.[1] It is not in the canonical version of the scriptures, but as we observed in an earlier chapter, the documentary authority for a number of stories which have been included in the New Testament is not as weighty as that of an equally large number which have been omitted. And this story, although it is not in the Bible, seems to me to bear the stamp of divine truth. It is a perfect exposition of a vital part of Christ's teaching.

The story is a pendant to the narrative which ends in the phrase 'The Sabbath was made for man, not man for the sabbath'. It is very short. It merely tells how Christ, after flinging out this challenge, walked along with his disciples.

And as he walked, he saw a man working on the sabbath. And he called to him:

Man, if you truly know what you are doing, you are blessed. But if you do not know, then you are accursed and a breaker of the Law.

I agree with Murry that these words are 'visibly authentic'. And even if they are the invention of some disciple, they are the invention of an inspired disciple who was filled with the true spirit of Christ. 'The man who knows God is above the Law; the man who is ignorant of God is bound by it, for to know God is to be so deeply

[1] See *The Life of Jesus*, by J. Middleton Murry.

one with Him that a man's will is God's will.' That is the doctrine which is implicit in this story. And that is our authority for daring to suggest that among the unrecorded sayings of Christ we might expect to find this profound truth — 'Marriage was made for man, not man for marriage'.

Which brings us back to the one and only answer to all sexual problems . . . Ask Christ.

'*Look upon him, till he look back upon us again. For so he will.*'

And if we thus look upon him, I believe that we shall find that there are some acts of sex, which might be regarded as monstrous in the eyes of the world, over which Christ would not waste a moment's scorn, and that there are other acts, done under the cloak of marriage and with a formula of complete respectability, which would bring forth his bitterest condemnation.

For Christ knew everything. Not only did he know everything, he *was* everything. He was the lily in the field and the wind in the branches and the song of the thrush in summer. He was the wave, and the rock on which the wave was breaking, and the spray which drifted like flying petals against the grey sky. He was the earth, and the sky that stares at the earth, and in the clouds he walked, though he left his footprints eternally on the dewy grass. He was the moonlight, and he was the lover on whose limbs the moonlight fell. How then could Christ, the heart of the world, be ignorant of any passion which was on the lips of the world, however strange that passion might be?

XII

If there are ragged ends in this chapter, you must forgive me. It would be easier to write the Lord's Prayer on a sixpenny piece than to compress so vast an amount of material — explosive material too — into a single chapter.

Let us abandon any attempt at literary form for a moment and deal with individual problems.

There are a great many charming people walking about the streets to whom the idea of an 'affair' is no more shocking than — let us say, a cocktail before dinner. You may think it odd to call such people 'charming', but as a matter of fact they are. They have all the graces, they are amusing, gay, and very often kindly. It merely happens that they are completely amoral. They wouldn't even think it necessary to defend themselves. If you told them that sex was keeping them from God they would open their eyes in polite astonishment and wonder if you had gone mad. At least, they would with *me*.

'Do you feel quite well, darling?' they would say.

'Grand, thank you.'

'No peculiar buzzings in the head . . . no ear noises?'

'No ear noises either, thank you.'

'You don't see any angels wandering about the room, by any chance?'

'Not at the moment.'

'Then, precious, what *is* it! You can't go about saying such odd things. Otherwise people will start rushing madly from the room whenever they see you.'

'I didn't say anything at all odd. I only said sex was keeping you from God.'

'Good Lord, he's at it again! Can't you *take* something? Aspirin — bicarbonate, something? In a minute I shall start to throw halfpennies at you, like they do in the Salvation Army.'

'Will you listen a minute?'

'Certainly not.'

'Only . . . five minutes . . . I won't be a bore, really.'

'I like *that*. You're being a crashing bore.'

'I won't be this time. Only damned rude.'

She pauses. 'Oh . . . that's a bit better. I like you when you're rude. Not when you're evangelical, but when you're rude. Perhaps . . .'

Before she has time to alter her mind, I begin. And this is what I say about sex, in the life of this young lady.

Firstly, it fills her with fears of every description. The chief fear is of growing old, which amounts to a mania with some people. More money is spent by women on various devices to keep them young than is spent on the combined army, navy and air-forces. (This, by the way, is not a statement at random. It may be verified by comparing the estimates for defence with the estimates for cosmetics.)

If you really analyse this fear, it has a sexual origin. This is, of course, very seldom admitted. 'It's a woman's *duty* to look attractive,' they say, glibly. Or they claim that 'it helps them in their business', or just say 'I like to look nice . . .' anything rather than the truth.

'But why the devil shouldn't they want to keep young?' you may ask.

I'm not saying they shouldn't. I'm only pointing out that the desire to look younger than you are is responsible for a great deal of unhappiness. At the extreme end of the scale it leads a woman to commit suicide. At the other end, it merely worries her, nags her, constantly upsets her. Every time she looks in the glass she is bothered. She doesn't say 'I look forty, and am forty, and what of it?' She says 'I am forty and I look forty and what has life left for me?'

That is one thing that sex does. It casts a shadow over the lengthening days, a shadow which in some cases leads women to the verge of the lunatic asylum and in others causes them an utterly disproportionate amount of worry and irritation.

And anything which does that may be described, without exaggeration, as keeping you from God.

XIII

'But darling, what do you want me to *do*? Go into a convent or what?'

'I merely ask you to face up to yourself.'

'Am I so awful?'

'Well, what do *you* think?'

'But I can't suddenly go about like a nun. Or can I?'

And then she probably says that I am making her feel miserable.

To which I answer by asking her a question. 'What happiness do you get out of promiscuous sex?'

Well — what? It fills you with the fear of growing old, the fear of losing the other person, the fear of being found out, the fear of scandal, the fear of missing somebody who is attractive, the fear of losing the money with which you increase your own attractions, the fear that you have lost the power to love, the fear that you have lost the power to be loved. Those are only a few of the fears with which a sexually promiscuous younger generation are constantly beset.

Is this not true?

Well, perhaps. . . .

All right. Let's ask the question again. 'What happiness do you get out of promiscuous sex?

A few fleeting moments, that are always marred by some discordant note. A few moments which will never come again, which you may eternally regret — bittersweet at best, but bitterer and bitterer as the years go by. And the maddening thing about it is that *you* gave the best of yourself to it. At least, you thought you did. You said your best things, did your best acts, were as charming as you knew how. For what? For a little music, and an hour's moonlight — if the moon were behaving itself. 'Oh . . . the damnable *mechanics* of all this sexual business,' you feel inclined to cry out.

All right. Why not cry out? Why not face up to it, to the question 'What true happiness do you get out of promiscuous sex?'

You scowl, and you mutter that you don't know. But you can't give it up.

And for this thing that you can't give up, you scheme and plot and weep and lie awake at night and beat your head against the wall. For *this* if you please! For this you tire yourself out and write wild letters and neglect your work and drink too much and end by cursing God!

Is it not at least arguable that promiscuous sex keeps you from God? And even if you put it on a lower scale, isn't it very obvious that it keeps you from your better self?

Of course to a great many good people these things will seem completely obvious. But I must remind you of a sentence I wrote earlier in this chapter — 'A large number of respectable parents in England and America would swoon with horror if they knew a quarter of the sexual life of their children in this year of grace.' It is for those people that I am writing.

We can now revert to the question of my imaginary friend, 'I can't suddenly go about like a nun, can I?'

This question brings us, once more, to the problem of 'sublimation'. And once more, to the example of Christ.

XIV

All problems are individual problems. When people are talking about the 'problem of sex' they usually think in terms of crowds. They don't realize that all that matters is their own case.

And when it is suggested that we should copy Christ's example and sublimate sex we reply, 'That's impossible'. Is it? Is it, that is to say, for *you*?'

I would suggest that you answer that question before reading further.

When you have answered it, let us see *how* Christ sublimated it. If you read the New Testament you will encounter a hundred ways in which he did so, and they are all ways of service. Perpetually serving, helping others, teaching them, giving of the very essence of his blood — these things leave a man little time or energy for the twisted and tangled by-paths of sex. Do you remember the case of the woman with the issue of blood? She touched him. 'Some virtue went from him.' It was the same always. Virtue was ever pouring from him, so generously that it was physically exhausting. Virtue went from him in that immortal dialogue with the Samaritan woman at the well. It went from him, over a period of three years, in the amazing training he gave to Peter. Into all the disciples he poured his spirit, and no man — and Christ was a man — can so pour his spirit without giving of himself physically, to the extent of exhaustion. And we must remember that Christ's spiritual reserves were not inexhaustible. He had drained them dry when he cried aloud from the cross, 'My God, my God, why hast thou forsaken me?'

In a million rooms, in countless cities, men and women have sunk to their knees, broken by the loves of this world, and cried out those same words in a sort of horrible parody of Christ. The cry has come to their lips because their little dusty paradise of desire has suddenly crumbled, and they are left shivering and alone. To this has the body led them, as it must always lead us, to shrunken husks, and vain echoes, and empty rooms where we cry alone. To this ultimate abomination of desolation must all desire conduct — it is written in the sands of every man's hour-glass. And all your earthly ecstasies die in darkness, as in darkness they arose, and all your music is broken on withered strings.

Such is the fate of the seed which is sown at random, with light fingers, over any pasture which may seem pleasant at the moment.

But the fruits of denial are, by a sublime paradox, infinitely sweeter than the fruits of desire. It is easy to laugh about all this, easy to mock, as I know well, easy to raise a shout from the crowd. The cat in the jester's bag will walk across any stage, and in this fantastically self-conscious year people's nerves are strung so tight that they will laugh when they should weep, and will weep when the band is playing the loudest.

But you know, and I know, that we are not very proud of that laughter. We are not very proud of the throbbing in our hearts which proclaims desire. Anybody can have desire. The point is, what shall we do with it?

It is for you to answer. Not for the world, not for your class, not for anybody else, but for yourself.

And if men would be guided by Christ I believe that they might make, of desire, a power that would change the world. A power that would make a garden of the foulest slum, and would turn every social discord into a perfect harmony. A power that would give to gold an unfading glitter, that would transform a million hatreds and suspicions into a universal love. A power, indeed, that would turn the world's bloody wars into a single shining peace.

But, you must remember, it must begin with you. For Christ's words were never spoken to the man next door. They were spoken to you. And it is in your heart that those words must vibrate, in music or in discord, in your soul that the seed must be sown, to bear what fruit you will.

CHAPTER III

CHRIST AND WAR

I

OR should the title of this chapter be 'Christ and Peace'?

That was the question that occurred to me as soon as the title was written. It is an example of the way in which Christ turns every problem upside down as soon as it is submitted to his scrutiny. And that is one of the excitements of Christianity. It gives you a new insight into the stories you read in the newspapers and a new echo to the conversation you hear in the train. Indeed, it sheds an entirely new light on all the activities of men. And most of the activities of men look so strange and so wild and so ugly, in this light, that we are forced to the conclusion that the number of true Christians in the world must be startlingly small, i.e. that instead of the millions on whom we conventionally congratulate ourselves, we shall be lucky if we find a few thousands.

In order that this statement may come home to you with its full shock, I am going to call to the bar, at once, an eminent Christian, and I am going to cross-examine him on his attitude to one of the world's greatest problems, the problem of war, in order to see how far he is in accord with the teaching of Christ.

To be particular, I am going to ask the present Bishop of London what he did in the great war. He will probably say:

Since writing this book a number of circumstances have contributed to change certain of my views on Christianity and Empire. Although the opinions stated in this chapter are still completely logical, modification is sometimes needed in their practical application. If further editions are called for I hope to make this point quite plain.

BISHOP. I did my duty.

MYSELF. As a Christian?

BISHOP. Certainly. And as a patriot.

MYSELF. We are not talking about patriotism for the moment.

BISHOP. The two are not incompatible.

MYSELF. I express no opinion on that. I merely point out that they are not the same things. And all I am asking is, did you do your duty *as a Christian?*

BISHOP (*loudly*). I did!

MYSELF. Thank you. I am now going to read you two extracts and ask you to recognize them. The first is from the Sermon on the Mount. '*Love your enemies, bless them that curse you, do good to them that hate you.*' Do you recognize that?

BISHOP. Yes, but . . .

MYSELF. Did Christ say it?

BISHOP. Yes, but . . .

MYSELF. Did it mean, anything?

BISHOP. Yes, but . . .

MYSELF. We will deal with your 'buts' in a minute. You have told us that Christ said it, and that apparently it meant something. We will now get on to the second extract. It is from one of your own speeches.

BISHOP. During the war?

MYSELF. Yes. The date is November 28th, 1915. The place is . . . Westminster Abbey, the home of Christ. I mention this in order that members of the jury may not be under the illusion that you were speaking at a recruiting station. This is what you said:

'*Everyone that puts principle above ease, and life itself*

239

beyond mere living, is banded in a great crusade to kill Germans, not for the sake of killing, but to save the world, to kill the good as well as the bad to kill the young as well as the old, to kill those who have shown kindness to our wounded as well as the fiends who . . .'[1]

BISHOP: Stop . . . Stop!

I think I'd better. I am not going to express any opinion on the matter. I am only going to ask you to contrast those two statements. Christ said 'Do good to them that hate you.' The Bishop said 'Kill those who have shown kindness to our wounded'.

Is the Bishop obeying his Master?

Is he?

II

It may seem unkind of me to single out the Bishop of London for these attentions. He is an old man, and I have every reason to believe that he is a kindly one.

But you see, I happen to take my Christianity seriously, and the churches apparently don't. And in case you think that the Bishop of London is an exception to the rule, here are a few more examples of the way in which our Christian ministers interpreted the message of the Man who said 'All they that take the sword shall perish with the sword'.

'Not without reason has the Christian Church ever loved to represent Our Lord's service *in military figures of speech*. Without shedding of blood there is no remission.'

[1] *The Potter and the Clay*, by the Right Rev. Arthur Winnington Ingram, D.D., Lord Bishop of London. Wells, Gardner, Darton & Co., 1917.

Believe it or not, these dove-like noises were emitted by the Bishop of Durham in Durham Cathedral, within two weeks of the outbreak of war.

Here is another:

'*God could stop the war, but in mercy abstains from doing so!*' This gem comes from the Rev. Robert F. Horton. He said it on February 4th, 1917, when the casualties had already run into millions.

'I beseech you, my hearers, to continue this war in the Christian spirit.' This entreaty is from the lips of the Rev. R. C. Gillie, speaking in Marylebone Presbyterian Church in 1915.

'God is calling us to hate, *and it is the duty of every true Christian to hate and to go on hating*, and to stifle any weak instincts of pity which the Devil may sow in his heart.' The man who said that is dead, and so I will not give his name, as he cannot defend himself. Not that he could defend himself if he were alive. Such statements are, of course, utterly indefensible. And yet they were made, *ad nauseam*, for four years on end from almost all the pulpits in Great Britain.

And exactly the same message of hate was being poured out by the pastors of Germany, the priests of Russia, of France, of Italy, and all the servants of Christ in every belligerent country all over the world. The vast majority of priests turned the cross into a recruiting emblem. Or perhaps it would be truer to say that as soon as war broke out they seized their national flags and hastily draped them over the cross so that nobody should feel uncomfortable.

Now do you see what I mean when I say that the

Q

Churches apparently do not take their Christianity seriously? And now do you feel inclined to agree that if this is the attitude of Christ's ministers, all over the world, towards the world's greatest problem, the problem of war, there can be very few Christians in the world?

For if Christ was anything at all, Christ was an uncompromising pacifist. Unless you admit that at once, fully, and without any sort of qualification, you and I must part company.

III

I am facing tremendous problems and levelling bitter accusations. It will help me if, instead of shooting these shafts at random, I have some sort of target. Which seems to be the cue for the entrance of the Bengal Lancer.

There lies before me a book entitled:

The Dogs of War
by
Major F. Yeats-Brown
(The Bengal Lancer)

Across the cover, in large black type, runs the words:

BEVERLEY NICHOLS CONFUTED!

Underneath the title is the quotation 'Pacifism is a Poisonous and anti-Christian Doctrine'.

Inside the dust cover, I read:

'Can there be Peace? Is war a thing of horror unrelieved? Mr. Beverley Nichols, author of *Cry Havoc!*, one of the most controversial and widely read publications of last year, answered "Yes" to both these questions. Major Yeats-Brown, who has acquired a vast circle of readers as the result of his *Bengal Lancer* and *Golden Horn*, with equal emphasis, "No". *Dogs of War*, a direct reply to *Cry Havoc!*, states an unanswerable case in a manner worthy of a great polemic, etc.'

And on the title page, in the Bengal Lancer's neat handwriting, I read, 'For Beverley, the onlie begetter of this little argument, from Y.B.' Which shows that we are still friends. I hope we shall remain so.

Now in *Dogs of War* you will find by far the most intelligent statement which has yet been written in defence of the thesis that Christ was *not* a pacifist. Every statement of Christ which can possibly be twisted into an argument defending war is given its full effect. (The most obvious example, of course, is the famous sentence 'I came not to send peace but a sword'.) Everything which Christ ever did which can conceivably serve as an argument for physical force is brilliantly adduced. (Again, the most obvious example is the turning of the money-changers out of the Temple.) And at the end of it all the author reaches the conclusion that 'Pacifism is a Poisonous and anti-Christian doctrine', and suggests that on whatever side Christ may have been fighting in the last war — was he pro-Roumanian or pro-Serbian, I wonder? — he was certainly not to be found in the prisons which housed the conscientious objectors.

That is the anti-pacifist interpretation of Christianity. It is most skilfully defended in *Dogs of War*. And in a few paragraphs the whole pitiful fabric of argument can be smashed to pieces.

Let us see how.

IV

I hope you will agree that this is a section of considerable importance. For hundreds of years, millions of 'muscular' Christians, 'militant' Christians, 'practical' Christians, and every other sort of Christian except that rare bird, the plain Christian unadorned, have been invoking the name of Christ in defence of every sort of war, whether it has been a war of defence or of aggression.

Their excuse for doing so has invariably been the same — a few texts, a few actions, recorded in the New Testament, and grossly misinterpreted. These texts and actions, needless to say form the basis of the Bengal Lancer's argument.

I think it high time that somebody put a stop to the blasphemous activities of these gentlemen, and I propose to do it now. That is why I said that this section is of considerable importance. If you cut it out, and put it in your pocket, you will no longer feel embarrassed when an army chaplain quotes at you the inevitable text 'I came not to send peace but a sword'.

And speaking of army chaplains, I think we might do worse than arrange our argument in the form of a little dialogue with one of these curious hybrids. There were magnificent army chaplains during the war, on both side of the line, all saying the same things, all subscribing to the same gospel of hate, and all believing that Christ was leading them. But that does not alter the fact that the profession of 'army chaplain' is a grotesque contradiction in terms. An army in action is an instrument of hate (please do not quibble about it), and a minister of Christ is an instrument of love. The phrase therefore is as illogical as 'undertaker-entertainer'. However, let us get on with our dialogue:

MYSELF. I think you are over-dressed.

CHAPLAIN. What do you mean?

MYSELF. I think you ought to take off either your parson's collar or your officer's uniform.

CHAPLAIN. You think they don't go together?

MYSELF. I *know* they don't.

CHAPLAIN. Because Christ was a pacifist?

MYSELF. Exactly.

CHAPLAIN. Supposing I proved to you, out of his own lips, that he was nothing of the sort, what would you do?

MYSELF. Apologize first. After that, I should probably shoot myself. Because you'd have taken away the only Christ I know.

CHAPLAIN. Sorry. But I'll have to take the risk. Now, you'll probably guess the first text I'm going to quote. (He turns to the 34th verse of the tenth chapter of St. Matthew.) In a resonant voice he reads: '*Think not that I am come to send peace on earth: I came not to send peace but a sword.*'

MYSELF. Yes. That is always the first point of attack, and the silliest.

CHAPLAIN. Well, anyway, Christ *said* it, didn't he?

MYSELF. Certainly.

CHAPLAIN. And how do you explain it?

MYSELF. I explain it by quoting the next verse.

CHAPLAIN. Eh?

MYSELF. You appear to have forgotten it. Very conveniently, if I may say so. For Christ went on to say, in the same breath, '*For I am come to set a man at variance against his father, and the daughter against her mother, and the daughter-in-law against her mother-in-law*'. What does that sound like to you? A world war?

CHAPLAIN. Well . . .

MYSELF. Sons, fathers, daughters . . . mothers-in-law . . . I repeat, was Christ referring to a 'patriotic' war when he talked about those people? Or was he referring to the bitter family divisions which had already been caused by his doctrine, and were increasing daily?

CHAPLAIN (*ironically*). I suppose that you are going to say that Christ meant the 'sword' to be symbolical.

MYSELF. You can either make it symbolical or place it in the hands of your mother-in-law. I don't care which. I only know what Christ said.

v

But the Chaplain is not impressed. He goes straight on to the second of his trump cards — the expulsion of the traders from the temple. (All these cards are, of course, used to the full advantage by the Bengal Lancer!)

'What do you make of that?' he demands. 'Christ

used force then, didn't he? Do you disapprove of his action? Or call it 'symbolic'? Or what?'

'Before I answer I'd like you to read the story to me.'

'Right you are.'

The chaplain, presumably, will turn to the gospel according to St. John, because this is the only gospel which tells us that Jesus used a whip. All the other gospels pointedly omit the whip. Still, we can let that pass.

This is what the chaplain reads:

'Jesus went up to Jerusalem and found in the temple those that sold oxen and sheep and doves, and the changers of money sitting; And when he had made a scourge of small cords, he drove them all out of the temple, and the sheep and the oxen; and poured out the changers' money; and overthrew the tables.'

The chaplain shuts the Bible with a snap. 'Well?'

I don't answer for a moment. I'm thinking of that scourge of small cords. It seems to me rather a slender instrument with which to slash to pieces the Sermon on the Mount. But it seems an even more slender instrument with which to attack a body of hefty Jewish traders. In fact it is quite impossible to believe that Christ intended to rely on those small cords for any practical purpose.

Just picture the scene. Whatever else you may call Christ (and he has been called a good many things in his time), you will probably find it difficult to call him a fool. Yet here he was, a man of comparatively delicate physique, marching with a scourge of small cords to do battle with an entire crowd of evidently unscrupulous men. It is no use reminding me that he had miraculous powers, because, for reasons best known to himself, he did not choose to employ them on this occasion, any more than he chose to employ them when they crucified him. For this occasion, he was a man, with only a man's force.

You agree? I humbly venture to hope that you do. Very well, then. If you agree, ask yourself this question, which I now put to our friend, the Chaplain:

'On what form of force did Christ really rely when he confronted that horde of angry men? On the scourge of small cords? Or on the moral force of his own indignation?

If you reply 'the scourge of small cords' I give you up. Anybody capable of making such a reply is capable of drawing an analogy between Christ, as he knotted the cords together, and a modern war-minister, as he enlarged his estimates for bigger and better tanks. The scourge of small cords was nothing — the scourge of his tongue was as a flaming sword. The physical force was negligible, the moral force was irresistible.

That is the lesson I draw from the story of Christ turning the money-changers out of the Temple. At the risk of sounding arrogant I would suggest that there is no other lesson that can be drawn, unless you are a fool or an armament-maker.

VI

But our Chaplain is not done yet. The ace of spades is still up his sleeve. It is the same ace of spades which was used with such effect by the Bengal Lancer. It happens to be the card which we can trump most easily of all, but he does not know that — yet!

He reads from the Bible again. Silently, slowly, in order to increase the tension, he turns to the gospel according to St. Luke. And he reads from it that amazing account of the Last Supper, which is not only a very great piece of literature but an even greater piece of psychological observation — although the significance of the observation apparently escaped the narrator.

This is what the Chaplain reads:

'And he said unto them ... *When I sent you without purse, and scrip and shoes, lacked ye anything?*
'*And they said, Nothing.*
'*Then said he unto them, But now, he that hath a purse, let him take it, and likewise his scrip; and he that hath no sword let him sell his cloke and buy one.*'

The Chaplain glares at me, triumphantly, as he reads the phrase about buying a sword. He finishes the quotation:

'*For I say unto you, that this that is written must yet be accomplished in me, And he was reckoned among the transgressors: for the things concerning me have an end. And they said, Lord, behold, here are two swords. And he said unto them, It is enough.*'

'It is enough,' repeats the Chaplain.
'What is enough?'
He scowls at me. 'You have, in those verses, a direct command to sell a cloak and buy a sword.'

'Yes. I think those are the most bitter words in history.'

'Bitter?'

'Ironic, then, if you prefer it.'

'You're not trying to prove that Christ was talking in symbols then?'

'I'm not trying to prove anything. I'm only asking you to take the story as it stands. And as it stands it is the wildest and most vitriolic example of sarcasm that ever fell from the lips of man. "Let him sell his cloke and buy a sword" . . . Good God!'

And then I lean forward and remind the Chaplain of a few more things that he has forgotten. I remind him that when Jesus spoke those words his whole intensely sensitive personality was tortured by the realization that even his faithful disciples had only grasped a fraction of his message. After three years of constant and arduous teaching, they still didn't know what it was all about. Only a few moments ago the sons of Zebedee had started a vulgar brawl about who should be the first in heaven, as though they were squabbling about who should have the best seats for a Cup Final. Confronting him was Judas, with wine by his side and the devil in his heart. Near Judas was Peter, and already Jesus, who must have been in a state of almost unbearable tension, had shot Peter to the heart with another bitter arrow, saying to him . . . *When thou art converted, strengthen thy Brethren!*

In the name of all that is sacred, what interpretation, save one of consummate irony, is it possible to put upon those words — 'When *thou* art converted'? They were said to Peter, of all people! And they were said with very good reason, for the hour of Peter's betrayal was at hand.

Not only the hour of his betrayal, but the hour of whole-sale callous neglect, when the disciples were to fall asleep at the one moment in their lives when they should have kept awake.

And now, with the effect of this cumulative evidence still fresh in your mind, remembering what had just passed and what was about to come, I would ask you to read, once again, the passage which the Chaplain quoted so glibly, ending in the words 'let him sell his cloke and buy a sword'. And I defy you to find in that phrase anything but a weary and infinitely pathetic gesture of a man who said to himself (because he *was* a man) — 'What is the use of talking to you any longer? Go your own ways. Do what you please. I've failed.'

And when you have read that, turn the page.[1] Turn it for two reasons. Firstly in order to see how swiftly his indomitable spirit recovered from this temporary depression. Secondly in order to hear the voice of the true Jesus, the Peacemaker, ringing down the centuries:

'And behold, one of them which were with Jesus stretched out his hand, and drew his sword, and struck a servant of the high priest, and smote off his ear.

'Then said Jesus unto him, Put up again thy sword into his place. For all they that take the sword shall perish with the sword.'

And with those tremendous words we will leave our Chaplain.

'All they that take the sword shall perish with the sword.'

[1] To Matthew xxvi, 51, 52.

If our Chaplain still tries to wriggle out of the argument I should suggest, once again, that he should also wriggle out of his parson's collar.

VII

'All right,' you may say, 'that sounds pretty convincing. If those are the best arguments that your army chaplain can produce, they obviously aren't worth producing. All the same, even if Christ was a pacifist (and unless we are to tear up the Sermon on the Mount he certainly must have been), I don't quite see what help that is to the average man. Can he help *me*, for instance, in my attitude to a modern war? Has he anything quite definite to say about it?'

To which the answer is 'Yes, he has something extremely definite to say about it. He has, in fact, the only answer. Because his approach to every problem of every kind is *through the individual.*'

The common soldier, the individual soul, and the individual body — this is the last thing of which the average warmonger thinks. It should be the first *and* the last. It certainly would have been with Christ. I have said this before, as clearly as I can say it, in *Cry Havoc!*, and I would like to quote a few sentences from that book:

'I believe that the discussion of war should *begin* with the personal agony of the soldier and should *end* with the political and economic frictions which result in that agony. In the same way I think that the discussion of poverty should *begin* with the realization of empty stomachs and squalid rooms and should end with statistics. If that sounds involved, I would merely explain, humbly, that I am trying to say that I should like to see a model of a hideously wounded soldier on the respectable tables of disarmament conferences, and I should like all parliamentary debates on unemployment relief to be carried out in the sombre and fetid atmosphere of a Glasgow slum'.[1]

Every problem, as Christ saw, is an individual problem, and the sum of the world's agony can be contained in a single soul. It is necessary to repeat this *ad nauseam*, because we are more and more apt to regard a soldier, not as an individual but as a thousandth part of a battalion. He is not a thousandth part of a battalion. He is John Smith of England, aged nineteen. And war means that John Smith is suddenly told by the army chaplains that God desires him to take up his rifle and blow out the brains of Johann Schmidt of Germany, also aged nineteen. Or vice versa. That is the beginning and end of the matter. There is nothing else to it. Needless to say this stark and simple theme of organized lunacy has many

---

[1] *Cry Havoc!*, first English edition, p. 12. This was deleted from some foreign translations, for reasons I have not been able to fathom, but was included in the Canadian edition, which was made compulsory in 8,000 Canadian schools. I wrote it nearly three years ago, and still subscribe to it. However, had I been writing to-day I should have inserted after the words 'personal agony' the words 'and spiritual degradation'. It is this aspect of modern war which Christ would, of course, most sternly condemn, the necessity for envy, hatred, and all uncharitableness, and the suppression of every decent instinct of pity and love. There is an astonishing school of thought, of which Ruskin was the most grotesque example and the Bengal Lancer the most plausible, which claims to find in war a stimulant of the manly virtues. We will have something to say about this later.

variations of horror — perhaps, for instance, John Smith may not shoot very straight and may only blow out one of Johann's eyes, or Johann may go mad, as tens of thousands of soldiers did in the great war, and run amok or cut his throat. Or perhaps they may both get a whiff of the same gas, if the wind changes, and may die a death to which the lowest animals should not be condemned. But all these variations are variations on the same theme — that John blows out the brains of Johann, who might have been his friend.

That is war, that is the whole of war, that is the only possible definition of war, and all the rest is bloody fake.

'Our honour has been affronted,' snarls an elderly diplomat. Will it be avenged by blowing out John's bowels?

'Our economic situation is desperate,' admits another. Will the economic problem be solved by shattering John's legs?

'We are fighting to defend civilization,' they cry. Will the world be more 'civilized' when you have blown off one of John's feet?

'We must expand!' By splintering John's spine? 'We must keep the flag of Liberty flying!' By blinding John?

When you put the reality, i.e. John's shattered body and twisted soul, against the sham, i.e. war, you instantly see how hideous and intolerable the sham is.

The thing is so self-evident that it would only be necessary to argue about it in a completely crazy world. But if you have the least doubt about Christ's attitude to the matter, ask yourself these questions:

Which would Christ regard as the reality, the frontiers of the whole of France or the soul of a single Frenchman? Which would Christ worry about — the freedom of the seas or the freedom of the soul? To whom would Christ say 'well done, thou good and faithful servant' — the men who wrote the various Hymns of Hate (and there were plenty of them in every language), or the men who suffered imprisonment as conscientious objectors?

Which would Christ regard as 'security', a strong air force or a national consciousness directed by God? Don't interrupt for a moment saying, 'But we *must* have a strong air force'. You may be right or you may be wrong. We are not discussing that. We are asking what Christ would have said.

You see, we are 'up against' something quite revolutionary when we ask Christ these questions. Very few people ever do ask them, and even they do not listen to his answer but manufacture one to suit their own convenience. That is why the churches all over the world were merely dusty annexes of the recruiting stations. They had not asked Christ. And again please do not interrupt by saying, 'Then was the last war all wrong? Should we have let Germany trample on us?' That really is not the point. I am not talking about what we think is right or wrong, but of what Christ thinks. And I must repeat, Christ's thought is *revolutionary*.

Can you see Christ with a national flag on his shoulder? With a bayonet in his hands? Can you see the fingers which healed the sick unscrewing a cylinder of poison gas?

Well — can you?

Don't tell me these are indecent questions. I know it. They have to be indecent because they are dealing with indecent realities. But they are realities. In the next war for civilization it will be the duty of a great many soldiers to unscrew a great many cylinders of poison gas. Many of those soldiers will call themselves Christians. Will they be doing what Christ would have done? You really must try to answer these questions, for the good of your own soul. Thinking that I might, in these words, have gone too far for publication, I turned to Tolstoy to reassure myself. Tolstoy was one of the greatest and most daring thinkers of the nineteenth century, although he is principally known, in the English-speaking countries, by his plays, which are comparatively non-controversial. Very few people have read his *Christianity and Patriotism*, a remarkable piece of genius, written in 1894. On page 44 of the English translation, published by Jonathan Cape, I find the following:

'A Christian state, to be consistent, ought, on entering upon a war, not merely to remove the crosses from the churches, to turn the churches themselves into buildings for other purposes, to give the clergy other duties, and, above all, to prohibit the Gospel — but ought to renounce every precept of morality which follows from the Christian law.'

I am not trying to shelter beneath the mantle of Tolstoy, but I admit that it is refreshing to find in this venerated figure so lusty an ally.

VIII

A few lines above I mentioned the 'conscientious objectors'. It is significant of the growing tension of the period in which I am writing that this phrase is once again gathering an aura of odium about it. It is somewhat ironical that this should be so, because the word 'conscience' is hardly despicable and the thing to which the conscience objects is utterly vile. However, the reason is not far to seek. People sneer at conscientious objectors because, as a rule, they know absolutely nothing about them. I will endeavour to shed a little light on the subject. And in that light I will ask you if you can deny that these are indeed sons of Christ in whom he would have been well pleased.

We will begin with Philippe Vernier.

Philippe is a young Protestant pastor, at one time secretary of the French Student Christian Movement. He is now serving a sentence of two years' imprisonment. He is kept in solitary confinement in a cell 9 ft. by 6 ft. and is experiencing terrible conditions. He is allowed almost no visits (except his relatives), no books of interest (except his Bible and three other books he brought with him), no writing paper (except what is required for his allowance of two letters a week). Most of his post is destroyed. A careful selection of letters and prospective visitors is made, with the object of permitting the minimum possible amount of encouragement and the maximum of discouragement in his attitude. He is now allowed to work. *This is the second term of imprisonment which*

Philippe Vernier, not yet 20 years of age, has suffered and he faces the prospect that, under the present laws of France, he may spend his life in such confinement until he is 50 years old.

These are not fairy stories but facts.[1] They are not culled from a savage country but from a highly civilized one. And remember, that Philippe is not refusing to carry arms in times of war but in times of peace. He is a brilliant young man. He might carve a great career for himself. He prefers to carve his name on the prison walls. It is a name which the cause of peace will not readily forget. And he sums up his creed by saying, 'I recognize the right of the land to condemn me, but I cannot recognize its right to take possession of my conscience, which does not belong to it. I believe that the French law which obliges all young Frenchmen to kill or to be prepared to kill, is contrary to the truth, and I do not believe that anything which is contrary to the truth can be good for my country.'

Well, Mrs. Colonel's Wife, you who were so generous with your white feathers during the last war, will you send a white feather to Philippe? It would be welcome, I am sure, in that little cell, 9 ft. by 6 ft., with the sun shining outside, and girls and boys laughing, and the song of the birds. Yes, I am sure your white feather will be very welcome, and you will know, as you send it, that you will have Christ's approval for your action. Come on, Mrs Colonel's Wife, write to Philippe, if only to prove how brave you are yourself.

[1] If you are interested in the case of Philippe, and thousands like him, all over Europe, please write to the War Resisters' International. Lord Ponsonby is the chairman and the address is Abbey Road, Enfield, Middlesex.

You have heard of Devil's Island. It is not generally regarded as a pretty place. Most people, in fact, would make somewhat strenuous efforts to avoid being detained there. They would certainly swear fidelity to almost any system, pay any oaths of allegiance and sacrifice their conscience completely. Well, after seven years of ceaseless effort the War Resisters' International has been able to bring back another man from the Penal Colony in Cayenne, French Guiana. He writes:

'After having been cut off from the world of living men during 19 years of exile for having resisted war; after having suffered numberless tortures more frightful than death; I have refused to allow hate to enter my heart, having retained in the midst of all these perils, the Ideal of Peace and love of one's fellow-men.

'In these critical times when the horizon is becoming dark, let us remain united in face of the peril of war; let us group together and resist in mass against those who, to obtain glory for themselves, would be responsible for millions of dead.

'Let us spread words of love and of peace; let us oppose by our non-violent, conscious and unshakeable resistance, all warlike activity, whose symbol is the flag bathed in unclean horrors, and which plunges humanity into blood, suffering, mourning and pain.'

There are many others still left in the Penal Colony out there. Well, Mrs. Colonel's Wife, there are some more white feathers for you to send. Indeed, now I come to think of it, you will need many pillowfuls.

You will need quite a number to send to Roumania, for

example, where there are hundreds of men (some of them ex-soldiers) who are resolutely refusing to have the least connection, directly or indirectly, with war. They are refusing *now*, remember, when there is no question of having to fight, when all they have to do is to wear a gay uniform and to spend a few months in camp. From the worldly point of view there is nothing very objectionable about that . . . I shouldn't mind the gay uniform myself, and I should enjoy the few months in camp exceedingly, if that were all it implied. However, rather than do these things, these men deliberately sacrifice their lives, now. There is no indulgence for such men. A first refusal is punished by a sentence of two years' imprisonment. They are made subjects of the bitterest mockery. The military tie guns to their arms and parade them in this state through the streets. The people spit at them, call them vile names. Any chance of a job, when they come out of prison, if they ever do, is of course hopeless. And as they are mostly poor men, and as their families usually reject them, they will presumably starve. In spite of this the authorities meet with absolute failure. The convictions of these war resisters are stronger than any violence the world can offer.

You will need white feathers for Jugo-Slavia too, where forty-five men are serving sentences of eight to ten years' imprisonment. Most of them have families dependent upon them, and the prison authorities do not hesitate to keep the war resisters well informed of the privations which those families are suffering.

As for Germany — well, I don't think you had better send any white feathers to the hundreds of young Germans who have refused to bear arms, in the piping times of peace. Black feathers would be more suitable. Big black feathers, like those which adorn a hearse. For, you see, the penalty of the war resister in Germany is likely to be death.

These young men know that. They are not moved by it. They stick to their guns, the guns they refuse to fire.

Contemptible, aren't they, Mrs. Colonel's Wife? Utterly contemptible. Any decent Christian woman, I am sure you will agree, would want to spit at such skunks.

XI

I make no apologies for being bitter and I make no apologies for being 'extreme'.

I use the word 'extreme' because I am sick and tired of compromise.

'Isn't this a little, er, *extreme*?' said a parson to me, after reading it.

'Isn't Christianity a little, er, *extreme*?' I replied.

Why not *face* it? Christianity *is* 'extreme'. It is the most wildly revolutionary creed ever preached. Why not admit it? I don't mind the man who tells me it is grand but won't work. I don't mind the man who tells me its all rot and won't work. Nor the man who tells me that he doesn't care whether it will work or not because he gets a thrill out of war. But I do bitterly mind the man who pretends to be Christian and at the same time tries to reconcile Christianity with war.

However, *are* we so sure that it won't work? Or perhaps instead of 'won't' I should have written 'wouldn't', because Christianity has, of course, never yet been tried. Are we so sure that if we were to apply this apparently dangerous and certainly revolutionary doctrine to world affairs, it would prove quite such a failure as its opponents suggest?

Let us see. It would be rather exciting. And we need not really be afraid of making fools of ourselves, in the name of Christ, because however hard we tried we could not equal the folly of those who have been making fools of us in the name of Mammon.

ANTI-CHRISTIAN. But you're mad! Run a country on the principles of absolute honesty, absolute purity, absolute unselfishness and absolute love ... why the very rumour of it would make the country bankrupt in a week ... sterling would collapse. ...

CHRISTIAN. Hasn't it collapsed already? Hasn't the mark collapsed? Hasn't the franc collapsed? Hasn't the rouble collapsed? Hasn't the dollar done something even more surprising than collapse?[1] Is there any such thing as financial security in the whole world?

ANTI-CHRISTIAN. But 'absolute honesty, absolute purity, absolute unselfishness ...' apply it to diplomacy. You'd have a war in forty-eight hours.

CHRISTIAN. And where did absolute *dis*honesty, abso-

---

[1] I refer of course to the closing of the American banks in the early Roosevelt days.

lute corruption and absolute selfishness lead us, please?
Those were the old forms of diplomacy. Did they prevent
the last war? Will they prevent the next?

ANTI-CHRISTIAN. But if you were no longer to rely on
force ... if you were absolutely defenceless ... any
country that was so mad as that would be at the mercy of
the world.

CHRISTIAN. Did Germany fail to rely on force in 1914?
Was Germany defenceless? I doubt it. Yet, she was at
the mercy of the world.

ANTI-CHRISTIAN. You are a danger to the community
... you and your Christianity.

CHRISTIAN. Yes? Will Christianity cause six million
young men to die in agony, with hatred in their hearts, for
nothing?

ANTI-CHRISTIAN. It's utterly unpractical. Look in your
newspapers.

Very well. We will look at them.

We will turn to one of those great British daily newspapers which claim to be Christian, and yet, unconsciously, work against Christ with all their might, year
in and year out.

On the principal page is an article by Sir Oswald
Mosley, the leader of the British fascists. I am not one
of those who belittle Mosley, nor do I regard fascism as
an unadulterated evil. It is a great movement which has
taken the wrong turning, and its opponents (among whom
I am the most vehement), would be better employed in
setting their own house in order than in throwing stones
at the fascist ramparts. However, that is by the way.

In this article by Mosley you will find a striking de-
nunciation of Englishmen who have been helping India
towards self-government. He writes: 'Many Empires of
the past have been taken away by force. The British
Empire will be the first to be given away.'

Remember that sentence, please. And now, say it
twice again, firstly to a political audience, and secondly
to Christ. What happens?

Well, obviously, when you say it to a political audience
the vast majority of men and women will share your
indignation. There will be sympathetic applause and
shouts of 'Shame'. It is a telling phrase; it suggests that
the speaker is a strong man who is out to protect his
country against the treachery of weak-minded poli-
ticians; a brave man, who will sacrifice himself to save
the birthright of the common people.

Now say it to Christ. 'Many Empires of the past have
been taken away by force. The British Empire will be
the first to be given away.'

No man dare set words on the lips of Christ, even in
imagination. But is it not certain that, in effect, he would
ask us, 'And why should you *not* give it away? Why do
you expect me to share your overweening determination
to cling to your earthly possessions? Have I ever said anything, at any time, in any place, which could lead you to
imagine *that*? Did I not say, "Lay not up for yourselves
treasures on earth"? Did I not say, "Whosoever will save
his life shall lose it"? Why then should you come to me
and expect me to feel a patriotic indignation because
England relaxes her hold on some parts of the earth,
which God gave to all men?'

'The British Empire will be the first to be given away.
The patriot *must* cry 'shame'.[1]

The Christian must answer, 'Why not?'

This is not a 'cooked' argument. It is an honest,
simple, and quite inevitable deduction from the evidence.
It is, admittedly, a startling deduction. But it is only
startling because we are not in the habit of taking our
Christianity literally. Christ's words meant this, that,
and the other, we say, they meant yes, no, or perhaps.
The one thing Christ did *not* mean, we comfortably
assure ourselves, is precisely what he said.

And when we take his words literally, the world turns
upside down.

x

These simple observations will seem to the average
reader so subversive, so 'Bolshevik' that even the most
hasty perusal is not enough. It never is, with anything
that Christ said. The sentences of Christ differ from the
sentences of ordinary men in this respect, that his words
have infinite echoes, that rise and fall over the remotest
hills of thought, carrying their music to the end.

Moreover, the Christian maintains that all his words
are workable. They are not merely patterns of abstract

[1] Patriotism was necessary to unite different nationalities into one state and
to make states strong for defence against barbarians, but since the light of
Christianity has inwardly transformed all these states alike, patriotism has become not merely superfluous but the one obstacle to that unity between nations
for which they are prepared by their Christian faith.'—Tolstoy, *Christianity
and Patriotism*, p. 70.

beauty, they are a practical guide to worldly policy. And not only are they practical, but they are universal. They answer *every* problem, for *all* time.

Let us see, therefore, how they apply in this case of the British Empire.

It will be admitted by all reasonable men that one of the principal causes of war is the struggle for colonial markets. It will again be admitted that many countries, notably Germany and Italy and Japan, regard with acute envy the widespread possessions of the British Empire. It will, finally, be admitted that another world-war would, in all probability, shatter what is left of civilization, and so weaken the Empire that it would be a prey to the forces of barbarism.

These are not suppositions. They are facts so obvious that apologies are needed for stating them.

Now, what would a Christian dictator of the British Empire do? (A 'Christian dictator' is, of course, a contradiction in terms, but the phrase will suffice for the moment.)

Presumably, he would call a conference of the Empire and say, very simply and concisely, 'Is it really for the benefit of the world that we should cling to every inch of the territory which, at the moment, we possess? Would it really be working against the world's peace if, in some cases, we handed our territories back to the races from whom we seized them, and in other cases, if we stood aside and allowed the pent-up populations of other powers to use them for their own people?'[1]

[1] This problem is so vast that it is, of course, impossible to argue it out in a single chapter. To hand over large tracts of Africa for the mere purposes of

The very possibility of such an occurrence is enough to cause the blood pressure of the press lords to rise to heights hitherto unrecorded by medical science. It is so obvious to them that all those red British patches on the world's map were painted by God, that the very thought of any of them being shaded with black or even faintly diluted with yellow is akin to blasphemy.

But we are not listening to the press lords, we are listening to Christ. And being simple, stupid people we are believing that Christ did not come to earth to tell a few pretty tales to children, but to tell the men of the earth how they ought to behave. And so let us close our eyes and put a finger on the map, at random. Where does it land? We will imagine that it lands on Australia. There's no reason why it shouldn't. Australia occupies a very considerable amount of the world's surface.

It is nearly as large as the United States. Its total population is less than the population of the City of London. It is an immense waste space on the face of the earth. All around it are countries gazing at it with longing eyes — countries who have no room to expand, with populations who might till its deserts and bring riches out of emptiness. But if you dare to suggest to the average Australian that a single Japanese labourer should be allowed to settle in 'his' country, he goes up in smoke.

exploitation by a rival capitalist power would certainly not be advancing the kingdom of Christ. It will seem to the normal man quite fantastic to argue that virtue is so infectious and God so powerful that such a gesture would bring its own reward, in that those who received the gift would themselves be 'changed' by it. This demands an act of faith, of which the world at the moment seems incapable. The only thing which might persuade the world to adopt Christ's teaching in this matter is an overwhelming realization of the fact that if they do not adopt it, the world is doomed.

It would be safer to tell him that you were about to blow up Sydney bridge.

'White Australia . . . white Australia,' that is the monotonous chant which echoes throughout the whole Australian press. It matters not at all that enormous areas of the continent are completely uninhabitable by white men. It does not even occur to them that these areas were very evidently created by God for the use of the coloured races. It only angers them when a great industrialist like the late Lord Leverhulme, on his last visit to Australia, proclaimed that the country could become the greatest sugar growing area in the world if the Australians would allow portions of it to be exploited by the Japanese. They won't allow it to be exploited by anybody but themselves. And as they are incapable of exploiting it themselves, the continent remains almost empty. A desert, kept empty by armed force. A desert, in whose emptiness are the germs of war.

Now you may call this situation politic, you may call it necessary, you may call it anything you like, but you cannot call it Christian.

And if you are a Christian, you cannot even call it common sense. The results of a war between England and Japan are too horrible to contemplate. On the other hand, the voluntary presentation to Japan of certain areas in Northern Australia is not horrible to contemplate at all. There is enough room in Australia for the entire population of Japan and the entire population of England, 'and then some'. Of course, if you have a 'war mind' you will instantly assure us that the Japanese would fortify the whole of the North Coast of Australia and use it as a base from which to destroy the British navy, and descend with fire and sword over the continent to pillage the rich cities of the South. And if enough men and women think such things of their neighbours, they will probably happen. They happened between 1914 and 1918, and they may happen again.

X I

The above is a thumbnail sketch of applied Christianity.

The Christian says that it will work.

The believers in 'keep what you've got by force', say that it is dangerous madness.

Now we cannot tell the 'keep what you've got by force' brigade that they are talking through their hats, because we are dealing not with facts but with suppositions. But we can tell them that they, of all people, are least qualified to criticize the Christian who wants to put his Christianity into practice. That they should presume to do so is a piece of colossal effrontery.

For they have *had* their chance. The Christian hasn't. For four years the 'keep what you've got by force' brigade had it their own way. From 1914 to 1918. They gave an unforgettable demonstration of their methods. They used all the force they wanted, they had an open field, there were no competitors, except a few war resisters in prison, whose voices were drowned by the roar of the guns and the cries of the wounded.

The 'keep what you've got by force' brigade have

shown us what they can do. They will never have a better opportunity of showing us. And as a result of their demonstration, whole stretches of Europe are white with grave-stones. Vast empires have perished, and those which remained are tottering. The victors no less than the vanquished have been impoverished for generations to come. The face of civilization is scarred for ever.

And so, if you belong to the 'keep what you've got by force' brigade you will, I trust, have the elementary decency to refrain from criticizing the Christian who suggests that *his* remedy, though it may be dangerous, is not likely to be as dangerous as yours. Otherwise we shall be compelled to observe that you remind us of a man with delirium tremens who tells us that we shall lose our virility unless we follow his example and drink a bottle of brandy a day. If that is the sort of virility which we are asked to cultivate we are quite prepared to lose it.

XII

I am not going to bore you, in this chapter, with long arguments on the theme of 'Is Force never Justified?' I am not going to consider the pros and cons of the League of Nations.

Nor am I so presumptuous as to attempt to lay down the law on the extent to which the British nation might share with other nations some of the immense territories of the Empire. I only know that the best way of consolidating those territories, of reaping real benefit from them, would be to change our attitude of exclusive possession and to admit, openly, that God created the world for man, and not only for the white man, nor for that particular sort of white man who speaks English.

I have been concerned with one thing and one thing only, the attitude of Christ to War. To me, and I hope to you, there can now be absolutely no question as to what that attitude is. How far he can copy it, is for every man to decide for himself.

I have no doubt whatever that a great many nice, respectable people will try to wriggle out of the alternative with which Christ presents them. They dare not proclaim themselves openly against him, partly because it would not 'pay' to do so, but principally because in spite of their wavering faith, they have a sneaking suspicion that 'there may be something in it after all', a haunting suspicion, half hope, and half dread, that on the other side of the dark curtain he still walks and lives, and beyond the grave his voice still echoes.

But though they dare not come out into the open and defy him, they skulk about in the shadows of their own creation, and deny, by their actions, the very essence of all that he taught. And to justify themselves they mutter, over and over again, 'you cannot change human nature'.

How many times have I heard that revolting lie quoted as an excuse for war. How many times, in the old days, did I repeat it myself!'[1]

You, too, have probably said, 'you cannot change human nature', at some time or other in your life. You

[1] Though I always qualified it by maintaining that you *could* change human *behaviour*, giving the abolition of slavery as an example.

have said those words, 'as a Christian'. And when you said them you didn't imagine that you were saying anything very remarkable. You would certainly have been quite indignant if anybody had told you that those words are a direct affront to Christ.

Yet, if you had paused to think, even for two minutes, you might have realized that the whole purpose of Christ's existence on this earth was to change human nature. And if you deny the possibility, you are saying to him, by implication, 'Go back ... we don't want you ... you're attempting the impossible'. Some brave men have said this, but it was the grey uniform of the atheist that they were wearing, and not the shining robes of the servant of Christ.

You *can* change human nature. No man who has felt in him the spirit of Christ, even for half a minute, can deny this truth, the one great truth in a world of little lies. You *do* change human nature, your own human nature, if you surrender it to him. To deny this is only to proclaim yourself as an uneducated fool. Read the life of Ignatius Loyola. Then, close the book and see if you can still say, 'you can't change human nature'. Go on. Do that. I challenge you!

Human nature *can* be changed, here and now.

Human nature *has* been changed, in the past.

Human nature *must* be changed, on an enormous scale, in the future, unless the world is to be drowned in its own blood.

And only Christ can change it.

That is the simple and irrefutable conclusion to which our stumbling footsteps have finally conducted us.

'All right,' you may say sarcastically, '*I* could have told you all that. You're just demanding a new world. That's all. You're telling us that everything in the garden would be lovely if countless millions of people were entirely different. You're not asking anything more than that! Very simple, I must say. But hardly new.'

Yes, it is very simple. And it is not at all new. It is nineteen hundred years old.

But perhaps it may be new to *you*. And certainly it must begin with *you*. For Christ's words, as I have said before, were never addressed to the man next door. They were always addressed to *you*. It is for *you* that the infinite comfort of them is stored, and for *you* that the breathless challenge is delivered.

Twelve men did quite a lot to change the world, nine-teen hundred years ago. Twelve simple men, with only the wind to bear them over the seas, with only a few pence in their pockets, and a shining faith in their hearts. They fell far short of their ideal, their words were twisted and mocked, and false temples were built over their bones, in praise of a Christ they would have rejected. And yet, by the light of their inspiration many of the world's loveliest things were created and many of the world's finest minds inspired.

If twelve men did that, nineteen hundred years ago, what might not twelve men do to-day? For God has now given us the power of whispering across space, of trans-mitting our thoughts from one end of the earth to another. What shall we whisper — what shall we think? That is the question.

With that, I must leave you. I reminded you of those

twelve, and what they did, because I believe that there are many more than twelve to-day who might follow their example. We who fight for peace are more powerful than we sometimes realize. We are so powerful that we shall win in the end, with the help of Christ.

Yes, we shall win. We *must* win. For the alternative is the death of the whole world.

Postscript to this Chapter

A fine Christian who read this chapter suggested to me that mere abstinence from war is not, *ipso facto*, going to better the world. 'There are worse things than war', he said. 'Sitting in an armchair drinking double martinis and wondering why all women bore one after the first two months . . . that's one of them.'

I agree. That is why after an exhaustive and exhausting experience with peace societies I came to the conclusion that however many times we might sign our names to pacifist manifestos, however many thousands of young men might take the pledge against active service in war, we were not really going to the root of the matter. The mere fact that fifty thousand young men are not going to be destroyed by poison gas is not, in itself, an advance, unless those same fifty thousand young men prove to the world, by their individual lives, that they are better alive than dead.

It all comes down to this, that for the lust for battle we have to substitute the lust for virtue — and no weaker word than 'lust' will do to express the mentality of those who 'hunger and thirst after righteousness'. This may seem an impossible ideal for those who perpetually think in terms of millions. But for those who, like Christ, thought in terms of the individual soul, it does not seem impossible at all. And even if it did, they would continue to fight for that ideal, saying, like Luther, 'Ich kann nicht anders'.

CHAPTER IV

CHRIST AND MONEY

I

THE scene is the Savoy Hotel, London. The time, a few years ago, when all the countries of the world were in the lowest trough of the 'depression'. The *dramatis personae*, Mr. J. H. Thomas, Secretary for the Colonies, and myself. The subject of discussion, money. The result of the discussion — 'nuts'. Or to spell it as it is pronounced by the vulgar — 'nerts'.

There have been many similar scenes, in expensive places and cheap places, with men whom the world has exalted and men whom the world has passed by, with orthodox financiers, with cranks, with communists, and always the result of the discussion was 'nuts'. Never was there a clearer instance of

> Myself when young did eagerly frequent
> Doctor and saint and heard great argument
> About it and about but evermore
> Came out by the same door as in I went.

As Mr. Thomas said to me: 'I've talked with all the economic blighters till I'm black in the face and I've come to the conclusion that none of 'em knows anything.' And since he had just come from a conference with the President of one of the most important banks in the world, and had also been constantly in the company of a brilliant economist of international reputation, his conclusions can hardly be regarded as hasty.

Of course, it did not really need Mr. Thomas to tell me that the financiers and the economists, of *all* schools of thought, were wallowing in a hopeless bog of ignorance. Before I left Oxford I had learned that the big money experts of the world were incapable of doing sums in simple arithmetic. I mean this quite literally. If you dig back into the dusty files of the Versailles Treaties you will find overwhelming proof of it. The most glaring example, of course, is the fact that the Allies demanded from Germany, in reparations, *more gold than there exists in the whole world*.[1] When I first worked this out, in five minutes on a half sheet of notepaper, I thought it could not possibly be true. But it was true. Germany was solemnly told, by the great financial brains of the world, that she must somehow hand over, within a stated period, *in gold*, a sum equivalent to all the gold in America, the British Empire, Europe and the rest of the world, and *then some*. It was about as sensible as ordering her to go and fetch the moon from the sky, and hand it to the King of England on a brass plate. And yet, this fantastic demand was supported, in the name of 'justice', and in the cause of 'prosperity', by all the economic master-minds of the world, in concourse assembled. And only a few odd little weekly magazines lifted timorous voices to suggest that, perhaps, the plan might not be as easy to work as it seemed at first sight.

[1] The ministers for the Dominions were the worst offenders. One Colonial Premier threatened to retire in a huff if reparations were fixed at less than fourteen thousand million.

This sounds like a story from *Alice in Wonderland*, but it is a strict record of fact.

These apparently irrelevant observations are made in self-defence, to guard me in advance against the criticisms of those economists who may tell me that I do not know what I am talking about. They may be right. All I would humbly suggest is that I know quite as much as they do.

And that Christ knew a great deal more.

And that though a hundred World Economic Conferences may meet to try to solve a hundred new World Economic Depressions, the assembled delegates will never arrive at any *practical* results until they print the words of Christ in large letters at the head of their programme, and until they incorporate his teaching, quite literally, in their decisions.

The only living financial brain which has a complete and detailed answer to all our apparently insoluble problems of supply and demand, unemployment, currency stabilization, rationalization and the like, is the master brain of Christ.

And until the financiers realize it, this world, like a ship laden with precious cargo, will continue to founder with all its riches untasted and untouched, because there were none who would obey the captain's orders.

II

Let us look at this world of money. The first thing we notice about it is that it is full of pessimists. The second thing is that they are not nearly pessimistic enough.

Big bankers say that 'they see very little hope of pulling out of the present depression for another ten years'. To which the answer is 'There is no hope, under the present system, of pulling out of the depression for another thousand years'.

Members of Parliament shake their heads and proclaim 'It's going to be a long time before we get unemployment down to a million'. To which the answer is 'Yes, but it's not going to be at all a long time before we get unemployment up to ten million.'

Consider this question of unemployment, which is the outward symptom of an incurable[1] economic cancer. Very few modern statesmen have the courage to say that there will *always* be at least two million unemployed in this country. Not a single one dares to suggest that within a very few years unemployment is likely to be doubled.

Most people are bored with statistics, and so we will illustrate our point with a story.

Did you hear about the Robot at the last World Fair at Chicago?

It was a frightening phenomenon for those who saw it. The Robot sat in a corner of the Fair, with steel impassive limbs. You pressed a button. The Robot lifted its arms, spoke and gave orders. And far away in a distant field, another Robot obeyed. The other Robot was seated on a plough, which it proceeded to direct over a forty-acre field, until the last furrow was turned. Without any human assistance.

---

[1] When I say 'incurable' or 'insoluble' it will not, of course, be forgotten that Christ has the practical cure and the only solution. But it would only lead to confusion if I constantly repeated this qualification at this stage of the argument.

All very simple. Just a little matter of pressing a button, releasing a gramophone disc, which communicated its orders by wireless.

And I understand that there are many enthusiasts in the United States who claim that the size of millions of fields should be standardized, so that they could all be ploughed at the same time, by a single man pressing a button in Washington.

Little stories like that — which are not fairy tales but facts — make one somewhat indignant with the dishonesty of the politician who glibly assures an audience of unemployed that 'the tide is turning' and that if only they will vote for his party the tide will turn so quickly that it will sweep them all back into jobs.

The tide will never turn. 'Rationalization' has gone too far. But it has not gone a hundredth part of the distance it will go.

Here is another little story which illustrates the point:

Two unemployed workmen were watching an immense steel excavator that was shovelling tons of earth out of a pit which was to be the site of a monster swimming pool. A dozen men, in all, were engaged in looking after the machine.

'Blimey, Bill,' said one to the other, 'if it weren't for that machine, there'd be five 'undred men on that job with shovels.'

'Yes,' said his friend. 'Or fifty thousand with tea-spoons.'

When you have subdued Nature with a vast machine, you are not going to tickle her with a tea-spoon.

And yet, we go on, searching for new markets, like a

lot of frenzied washerwomen scrubbing each other's
night shirts, when there aren't even enough night shirts
to go round! The blindness of the economists is baffling
to the average intelligent man. They go on shouting
'New Markets! New Markets!' when they can hardly
hear themselves speak for the roar of the machines which
are flooding *all* markets.

Here is another story which may make you think. A
conversation I had with Henry Ford, before the 'depression'. It illustrates the strangely constricted mind of
the average great industrialist, who sees in New Markets
the panacea to all problems. We talked in this fashion:

FORD. I shan't be content till every workman in
America has a Ford car.

MYSELF. And when he has?

FORD. We're already starting mass production in
Europe.

MYSELF. And when everybody in Europe has a Ford
car?

FORD. I shall start on the negroes in Africa.

MYSELF. And then?

I forget Ford's answer to the last 'And then?' The
only logical answer, of course, would be that having sold
Ford cars to everybody on this earth, he would have to
start a commercial conquest of the moon. Indeed, there
is a good H. G. Wells fantasy in that idea. A trade war
among the planets, compelled by the inevitable exhaustion
of the markets of this world, and ending in the equally
inevitable war of men and guns, waged in the sacred
name of Profit.

I have splashed the beginning of this chapter in somewhat lurid colours because it is vital that you should realize that unemployment has come to stay. Until you realize this, you are living in a fool's paradise.

And until you realize the monstrous paradox which lies in the penalization of the workless for not working when there is no work to do, you will not be conscious of what is going on around you.

I could write reams of dull stuff about this, stacked with statistics from the most irreproachable sources, but it would only give me a headache and send you to the movies. And so we had better put the situation in tabloid form. . . .

Firstly, the machine has developed, in the last few decades, out of all recognition, and the Age of Leisure, so long dreamed of by philosophers, has actually arrived.

Secondly, an outworn system of ethics (*not* based on Christianity) has affixed to the Age of Leisure the ugly label of the Age of Unemployment.

Thirdly, an equally outworn system of banking and credit (not based on Christianity but chained to gold), has clanged the gates of the worldly paradise which is opening before us, and has denied to man (because he has not the requisite amount of gold in his pocket) the right to participate in the benefits of that paradise.

You can read Keynes and McKenna, you can bury yourself in the lore of Social Credit, you can ask the Governor of the Bank of England out to dinner, you can go back to Adam Smith and paper your bathroom with the supplements to the *Financial Times*, but you won't get much more out of it than that.

A world of plenty. The plenty created by the machine. The plenty denied by the mechanism of credit. The result — millions of men standing at street corners all over the world, swearing at God and man in countless dialects.

That is the problem which baffles all the great brains of the world. And the problem which Christ, in a single, lovely phrase, can solve.

The single, lovely phrase is written in the sixth chapter of St. Luke. 'Give, and it shall be given unto you; good measure, pressed down and shaken together and running over, shall men give into your bosom.'

I V

'What, is *that* all? A sort of indiscriminate charity?'
'No, that's not quite it.'
'Well, a sort of socialism?'
'No, that's not it either . . .'
'Well, what *is* it? I thought you said he had a detailed plan. Up till now you don't seem to have suggested anything very practical.'

You will see that Christ has a detailed plan, if you go on reading. In the meantime, just as we requested the anti-Christian warmonger to have the elementary decency to refrain from calling Christ's attitude to war 'unpractical', so we will request the anti-Christian economist to refrain from calling his attitude to finance 'unpractical'. You may think that Christ gave a lot of foolish commands, but you can hardly suggest that he ever gave commands quite as foolish as those which the upholders of the capitalist system are giving all over the world to-day.

Among the things which Christ did *not* say are the following:

'Burn this cargo of fresh flowers! Destroy this field of wheat! Throw this ship-load of coffee into the sea! This is a world of plenty, but we must not touch it! Do not pick up the fruit from the ground! Let it rot!'[1]

Christ never said anything quite as silly as that. The capitalists are saying those things every day. And their words are being obeyed.

So however foolish you may think the commands of Christ, you can hardly suggest that they are as foolish as the commands of the modern financiers. Outside the pages of *Alice in Wonderland* such pure folly does not exist.

'All right, all right,' you may say, 'that may be true, but we're getting impatient. What would Christ *do*? Would he, for example, be a socialist to-day? Can't you answer *something* definitely?

We can and we will. And I think that the first glimmerings of the great Christian plan for world reconstruction will be found in an exhaustive answer to this question: 'Was Christ a socialist?'

---

[1] Thousands of tons of fruit are allowed to rot every year in the colonies because it is not 'economically' profitable to transport it to England. At the same time millions of tons of shipping lie idle, which could transport the fruit, and thousands of merchant seamen are unemployed, who could man the ships. And finally, millions of people want the fruit. Yet, the fruit remains to rot!

Bernard Shaw would answer with an emphatic 'Yes'. Many socialists would answer with an emphatic 'No'. Both would be wrong.

Which, I admit, is enough to make the man who wants clear-cut answers throw down this book in a huff. Yet the paradox is true, and we will try to prove it as quickly as possible.

We can begin to do so by examining a letter which I have recently received from a prominent young socialist in Scotland. It seems to me an exceedingly foolish letter, but as the man who wrote it makes quite a loud noise in the North, it is presumably typical of a certain school of thought.[1]

'*Was Christ a Socialist?*' writes my friend. '*Of course not! No decent Socialist can be a Christian, because the very essence of Christianity is Individualism, which is the very antithesis of Socialism. Christianity says to the people, Live hereafter; Socialism says to the people, Live now!*'

I ought not, perhaps, to pause to examine these statements. It ought to be enough to put a tick against them to register the fact that they represent the considerable antipathy in which Christ is held by a certain section of socialist opinion. And yet I cannot resist the temptation to expose the tangles of muddled thought and muddy philosophy which is revealed in them. After all, we want to know what Christ really felt about money, and it may be clearer to us after we have thrown a little light on to the darkness of one socialist's mind.

[1] I trust that no readers will imagine that I have concocted this letter out of my own head. As they say in advertisements, 'The original testimonial can be inspected on demand'!

If you read the beginning of his letter again you will
see that he says, in effect, 'Live now, but not as an individual!' That is his interpretation of socialism, and it
seems to me such a weird ideal that I cannot even begin
to understand it.

How *am* I to live, if not 'as an individual'? What is
life worth, if it is not 'individual'? Is not my sorrow my
own sorrow, and is not my joy my own joy? No? Then
I must do everything with the crowd, must I? I must
reserve my weepings for public places, and my jubilations
for summer holiday camps of the Third or Fourth or
Fifth 'International'?

'Live now, but not as an individual!' That is what my
socialist friend said, and I am not twisting his words by
a fraction of an inch. I should like to hear him say it to
a mother in child-birth. To a great composer, finishing
his symphony. To a nice little shabby servant girl,
clutching her lover with sticky hands, in the Park. Oh —
the dreary visions of Russian barracks, of communal
kitchens, of 'impersonal' marriages and Robot love which
that phrase suggests!

Of course Christ was an individualist. Nobody outside
a lunatic asylum ought to be anything else. And the only
reason why certain people condemn Christian individualism is because they confuse it, somehow or other,
with the abuses of the capitalist system. That is an
example of such confusion of thought that it can only be
corrected by teaching the writer of the letter the multiplication table.

Another example of confusion is to be found in the
phrase 'Christianity says to the people Live Hereafter,

Socialism says to the people Live Now'. If the writer of this sad little sentence had read the New Testament he would have realized that what Christ really said was 'Live fully now, in order that you may live fully hereafter'. And by living fully he meant what he said, for no man can live fully who does not pour out his life for others. Christ knew that the grey days in a man's life are those in which he has been shut in with his own soul, barred by the invisible bars of his petty egotism. He knew that the golden days were those in which there had been sacrifice, an outpouring of the spirit, a sharing of earthly benefits. He who desires to gain happiness must first give it. That was his message, of such sweet cleanliness that it shines like a morning flower through all the world's dusty prose. And when somebody writes to me and blandly suggests that Christ demanded the impoverishment of this life in order to attain a spurious enrichment of the next . . .

To accuse Christ of belittling this life!

Christ, for whom the lily flowered in words of eternal consideration! Christ, for whom the well water sparkled like diamonds, flashing its colour through his brain, and through the world in a myriad facets. . . .

However, we must hold on to ourselves. The only merit of this little outburst is that it may have slightly cleared the air.

We will quote another phrase from our socialist's letter, and then we will sum up our progress to date.

He begins by quoting a poem which is very popular in communist circles:

'Peace on Earth' 'twas said;
We sing it
And pay a million priests to bring it;
After two thousand years of Mass
We've got as far as poison gas!'

And then he goes on to say:

'Christianity, by denying the Social Man and exalting in his place the Individual Man, destroyed social Harmony. It was therefore inevitable that Christianity should find its natural habitat within the politico-economic framework of a system of society based upon individualism. "Save your own soul" reads the same to me as "look after number one".'

There would be no excuse for quoting this nonsense if it were not typical of a great deal of the stuff which is preached day in and day out, by socialist opponents of Christ. You may pooh-pooh these people, you may say that they are not worthy of any man's attention. I don't agree. These lies should be stopped before they are allowed to spread any farther.

The little Glasgow socialist writes:

' "Save your own soul" reads the same to me as " look after number one".'

That is an 'intelligent', up-to-date socialist criticism of Christianity. We will answer it by a few words of Christ:

'Whosoever will save his life shall lose it.'
'Lay not up for yourselves treasures on earth.'
'Ye cannot serve God and mammon.'
'It is easier for a camel to go through the eye of a needle than for a rich man to enter into the kingdom of God.'

Well, my little Glasgow socialist, do you want any more? Do you still think that Christ was a 'contemptible lackey in the halls of capitalism'? Or are you beginning to realize that you have got hold of the wrong end of the stick?

You see, Christ, as I have said before, turns everything upside down. He certainly said 'save your own soul', and it seems to me, at the lowest estimate, a very sensible thing to say. I am not at all ashamed of wishing to save my own soul. It seems to me as obvious an instinct as the desire to save my own life if I trip into the Thames.

It might also be claimed that Christ said 'look after number one'. But if we make that claim, we must interpret it rightly. To Christ, 'looking after number one' meant, first and foremost, looking after number two. For which obvious epigram I would refer my Glasgow friend to the words 'Love thy neighbour as thyself'. An injunction which I fear I am in danger of forgetting.

V

Let us now sum up our progress to date:

Christ, as a certain section of the socialists are only too eager to proclaim, was not a socialist in any accepted sense of the word, because he was an acute individualist. To him, any act of sacrifice to be of any value must be *voluntary*.

'But surely, you're quibbling,' you may say. 'What about his advice to the young man who wanted to inherit eternal life? Didn't he say "Go thy way, sell whatsoever thou hast and give to the poor?" Doesn't *that* sound like socialism?'

'On the contrary it sounds less like socialism than anything you could possibly mention.'

'I don't understand.'

'Listen. When do you feel most charitable . . . when you pay your rates or when you give a pound to a beggar?'

'Well obviously, when I give the pound to the beggar. Paying rates isn't charity . . .'

'No. But it's a form of socialism. All taxation is. And taxation may be necessary, but you can hardly say that it sweetens the soul or disciplines the spirit. Obeying a law, with the knowledge that you will go to prison if you break it, is common sense, that's all. *Now* do you begin to understand?'

This distinction is fundamental. It is also of such simplicity that a great many people have not grasped it. And among these people is our old friend, Bernard Shaw.

Shaw is among the most generous men living. He is far nearer to living a truly Christ-like life than the great majority of his fellow citizens. If the world has not realized this it is due to the fact that he has always obeyed Christ's injunction 'Take heed that ye do not your alms before men, to be seen of them . . . do not sound a trumpet before thee, as the hypocrites do in the synagogues'. The only time on which Shaw sounds a trumpet is when he tells us how much money he has made. When he gives it away, he holds his peace.

All the same, Shaw is utterly wrong to turn Christ into a Fabian official, which is really what he does. He says that Christ's advice is 'impractical', because it really amounts to 'advising you to become a tramp'. He maintains that the teaching of Christ can only be administered to civilization through a fabric of laws and ordinances, i.e. through socialism.

You see? The old pitfall again. We are to become Christian by *law*, by signing forms, by subscribing to one particular brand of economics. All *voluntary* sacrifice, such as Christ demanded, is to be wiped away. Why? Because, Shaw says, it wouldn't work. He puts it like this:

'Even in Syria in the time of Jesus his teaching could not possibly have been realized by a series of independent explosions of personal righteousness on the part of separate units of the population. And what could not be done in Jerusalem cannot be done in London, New York, Paris and Berlin.'[1]

In other words, you cannot change human nature. It is unchangeable, beyond redemption.

In other words, again, Christ's command to the young man who had great possessions was a foolish command. It was 'advising him to become a tramp'. It would do more harm than good. (To whom? one wonders. To the young man? Or to the people who were benefited by his alms?)

In other words, once more, our salvation lies, not in the Bible, but in a system of economics. In one system of economics and one only, says Shaw.

And as he says this, we seem to remember that the sands of time are littered with the literature of economic systems which, in their time, were the one and only solution. All those systems have long ago been blown into the sea. The

[1] Preface to *Androcles and the Lion.*

one system that remains is the one system that has never been tried. Because, we are told, 'it would not work'.

Wouldn't it? Let us see.

VI

It is now generally admitted, in every country, by men of every school of thought, that one of the most potent causes of the disastrous economic depression into which the world has plunged, is the burden of war debts.

You will find very few people who will deny it. You will find very few people who will even deny that the debts have done as much harm to the creditors as to the debtors, and have been equally pernicious whether they were paid or left in abeyance.

They have disrupted trade, poisoned international relationships, and instead of creating wealth, have destroyed it.

Now would you turn to the sixth chapter of the revised version of St. Matthew, the twelfth verse. Here you will read some words which may not be entirely unfamiliar to you:

'Forgive us our debts, as we also have forgiven our debtors.'

Now please do not let there be any quibbling about this. If you are to swallow your Christianity at all you must swallow it neat. You must refrain from diluting it with any patent medicines which may be recommended to you by any persons whatsoever.

Here is a plain injunction to forgive our debtors. We know the meaning of the word 'forgive' and we know the meaning of the word 'debtors', and so the injunction can hardly be regarded as obscure.

If this plain and practical piece of advice had been printed, in large black type, on the blotting paper of every delegate of the allied nations at the Conference of Versailles, and if it had been followed, the world would have been saved incalculable hardship and misery.

'But . . . but that's *impossible*,' you may say. 'Why . . . you'd be striking a blow at the very foundations of credit, if you just let people off their debts.'

Please don't make me laugh. If you'd been in Wall Street in 1929 you'd have realized that somebody was striking a devastating series of blows at the 'foundations of credit'. But it wasn't Christ. If you'd been in Germany during the inflation, or in France when the franc was sinking, or even in England during a good many recent crises, you might agree that 'the foundations of credit' were so shaky that it didn't need Christ's assistance to undermine them.

You can argue till you are tired, you can turn this way and that, but you won't alter the facts, which are:

Firstly, that Christ told us to forgive our debtors.

Secondly, that we did not forgive them.

Thirdly, that every sensible man in the financial world realizes that we ought to have forgiven them.

Those are facts. They seem to me, unless I am as blind as a bandaged bat, to lead to the conclusion that Christ, on one great economic problem, was right.

And if he was right on one great economic problem,

when all the rest of us were wrong, is it not conceivable that he may have been right on another?

Once again, we will see.

VII

If you will turn back to the little tabloid analysis of the world's economic troubles which we gave, earlier in the chapter, you will find that we discovered that we were living in a world of plenty, created by the machine, but that we were debarred, by an outworn system of ethics, from participating in that plenty. The outworn system of ethics is one which attaches virtue to work. It was formulated in the Age of Scarcity, when there was a very obvious virtue in work. It is creakingly out of date in the present age, when the machine has obviated the necessity to work for a very large percentage of the population.

How criminally stupid this system of ethics really is may be best illustrated by a dialogue between an ethical gentleman and an 'unemployed'.

E.G. You can't have this loaf of bread unless you pay for it.

UNEMPLOYED. But I haven't any money.

E.G. Then you must work, and make some.

UNEMPLOYED. All right, *let* me work.

E.G. *Let* you work? Certainly not! My machines do that much better than you can.

UNEMPLOYED. But if I'm *willing* to work, wouldn't that be the same thing?

E.G. Not at all. I'm not interested in what you are *willing* to do. I'm interested in what you *do*. And what you must do, before you can have this loaf of bread, is *work*.

UNEMPLOYED. But you've told me you don't *want* me to work.

E.G. Of course I don't.

UNEMPLOYED. Then what am I to do?

E.G. *Work!*

UNEMPLOYED. But how?

E.G. Don't ask *me*! I'm worried enough already with all these loaves of bread on my hands, and nobody to buy them.

UNEMPLOYED. We'd take them off your hands all right, if we had the money.

E.G. (*exasperated*). Well then, go and *work*!

There, in all its tragic simplicity, is revealed the brutal predicament of millions of men to-day. The utter stupidity of it has never been more bitingly revealed than by Shaw, with whom we find ourselves, for once, in complete agreement. I would like to quote him because there are still many people who cling to the idea that work is the only claim a man can have to money, and that if men do not work they have no right to money:

'Was ever so idiotic a project mooted as the estimation of virtue in money?' writes Shaw. 'The London School of Economics is, we must suppose, to set examination papers with such questions as 'taking the money values of the virtues of Jesus as 100, and of Judas Iscariot at zero, give the correct figures for, respectively, Pontius Pilate, the proprietor of the Gadarene Swine, the widow who put her mite in the poor-box, Shakespeare, Mr. Jack Johnson, Sir Isaac Newton, Palestrina, Offenbach, Sir Thomas Lipton, your family doctor, the Archbishop of Canterbury and the common hangman.'

I do not think you can put it clearer than that.

Please do not think that Shaw and I are advocating a sudden universal lethargy or suggesting that a solution to the world's problems will be found in the command 'Down Tools'. All we are doing is to face the fact that for millions of men the command 'Down Tools' has already been given. It has been given by the machine. And it is a command that will never be revoked.

VIII

'But what has this to do with Christ? How can *he* get us out of this mess? By making us all put our hands in our pockets and give to beggars in the street? That's not very scientific, is it? Hasn't he anything more clear-cut than that to tell us?'

Yes, he has. But how on earth I am going to get it into a single book, let alone a single chapter, I don't know.

We had better illuminate this passage with one of his shining sentences. It is always a help to recall a phrase of Christ's, even if you have only lost your temper or sprained your ankle. And heaven knows, we need his help here.

Remember, the problem is 'a world of plenty, with the plenty denied to men, firstly because they have not the money tokens to pay for it, secondly because these tokens can only be obtained by work, and thirdly because the work does not exist.'

Turn to the sixth chapter of St. Luke, verse 34. 'And if ye lend to them of whom ye hope to receive, what thank have ye? For sinners also lend to sinners, to receive as much again . . . *Lend*, hoping for nothing again'.

We scratch our heads. There seems the glimmering of an idea here — but we're not quite sure what it is. Somehow, it seems to switch our thoughts to the Bank of England and the large joint stock banks. We're not at all clear about it, but we do know that they have a complete monopoly of the creation of money and credit. And we also know that they are very far from adopting the doctrine — 'Lend, hoping for nothing again'. Sometimes, after an interview with our bank manager, we have a shrewd suspicion that he is hoping for more than he will get.

We rise, and walk to the window. We throw it open — a breath of fresh air will do us good. Somewhere in the distance, let's say, a church service is going on. (All right, I know it's only a supposition, but it's not an impossible one.) We listen. And faintly, down the lonely street, there drift the words of the old hymn:

> In vain with lavish kindness
> The gifts of God are strown
> The heathen in his blindness
> Bows down to wood and stone.

We stare into the gathering darkness. The words echo in our brains — 'Bows down to wood and stone'. Slowly, we close the window. We go back to our chair.

All sorts of phrases are muddled up in our mind — 'Wood and stone' — 'the joint stock banks' — 'lend, hoping for nothing again' — 'the age of plenty, credit denied'.

And suddenly, as though it were written in letters of flame in the dancing fire, we see the solution. And once again, Christ has given it to us.

IX

The solution of the problem lies in that word 'credit'. The world is staggering under a burden of debt. 'Inflation' will not lighten the burden; it will merely increase it. 'Economy' will not lighten it. It will merely restrict purchasing power, and cause us to slow up, still further, the machines which are waiting to give men the natural riches of the world.

Nothing will relieve that burden except a new interpretation, throughout the whole financial fabric of Europe and America, of the vital word 'credit'. To the average financier, 'credit' means *doubt*. To the Christian financier, 'credit' means *doubt*. To the Christian financier, 'credit' should mean *faith*. And not only should it mean *faith*, but it should mean the sort of faith which is entirely dissociated from the hope of reward. In other words, we have to face the fact that sooner or later the great financial institutions of the world will be compelled to grant *credit without interest*.

We have the clearest commands from Christ to this effect in the words '*If ye lend to them of whom ye hope to receive, what thank have ye?*'

What thanks, indeed? We have lent of whom we hope to receive, and as a result, we cannot lift our hands to pick up the earth's riches because they are laden with the chains of debt.[1] We have lent of whom we hope to receive, and as a result, the only people who are quite certain of themselves in the financial world are the bankrupts. We have lent of whom we hope to receive, and as a result, capital flies from country to country, seeking 'security', from funk-hole to funk-hole, like a frightened rabbit, trying to escape from the just wrath of the hound of heaven.

It is obviously beyond the scope of this volume to indicate the working out, in practice, of Christian economics. All we can do is to reiterate three points:

Firstly, that there is no other way, no other hope of 'security'.

Secondly, that the granting of the requisite credits, among individuals, corporations, and nations, is a spiritual problem, and nothing else, for the simple reason that Europe, materially speaking, has almost everything that Europe wants. Europe is not a desert. It is not swept by devastating storms. It is not ravaged by earthquakes. It is not inhabited by ignorant savages, untutored in the technique of agriculture and engineering. It is merely inhabited by fools.

Thirdly, that the change, when it occurs (as it must inevitably occur unless we are all to tumble, snarling and hungry, into a grave of our own digging), will be brought

---

[1] The whole tragic farce of Anglo-German loans, beginning with greed instead of charity, and ending inevitably in a moratorium, is a biting commentary on Christ's words.

about by the changing of individual lives, through Christ, on an enormous scale. If you think this is impossible, then you are indeed living in a nightmare world, and there is little hope. If, on the other hand, you think it possible, you are faced with the greatest adventure of your life.

For my own part, I *know* that it is possible, and I know that I must labour to make it go.

x

And now let us leave this tangle of problems and look forward, for a little while, to the world of money as it might be if Christ were directing it.

I have said before that one of the most exciting things about Christ is that he turns the world upside down. He alters things, not only in degree, but in kind. He has the power to turn what is apparently an unmitigated evil into a limitless good. And nowhere is this more apparent than in the 'problem' of unemployment.

'Unemployment' was not in Christ's dictionary. It would have been a meaningless word to him. It should be a meaningless word to us, instead of the harrowing nightmare that it is. The idea of 20,000,000 unemployed, in this country, is admittedly depressing. But it is depressing only because of the word 'unemployed', which is the creation of economic sin, which, in its turn, is the fruit of spiritual barrenness.

Let us indulge in the luxury of a moment's wild optimism. Let us imagine that there is a new spirit in Europe, that war ceases, that men take full advantage of the machine, and that a Christian interpretation of credit allows fifty per cent of them to share in its benefits. What happens?

Well, before we can suggest what would happen a number of highly respectable persons will have raised their voices in horror, because of the ancient fallacy that 'work', *qua* work, is essential to salvation. These are the persons whose favourite text is 'The devil soon finds work for idle hands to do'. They never seem to reflect that the word 'devil' might easily be struck out in favour of the word 'God', and that the phrase 'idle hands' might be interpreted to mean hands that were not chained by perpetual drudgery.

However, people who think like that are not impressed by generalizations. They want facts. So let us return to our favourite device of the dialogue.

'What . . . twenty million people doing *nothing*. . . '

'No — twenty million people doing what they want to do, instead of what they are told to do.'

'They'd all be completely degenerate in a year.'

'Are you completely degenerate?'

'I beg your pardon?'

'You do what you want, don't you? Has that destroyed your soul?'

'My dear fellow, *I* am educated. I have a multitude of interests . . .'

'Well, why shouldn't they be educated too? Why shouldn't they have a multitude of interests?'

That is the sort of argument that you may expect to have with the respectable £5000-a-year man.

Here is the argument you will have with quite a number of 'moralists'.

'A certain amount of really hard and even unpleasant work is vital for building up character.'

'Quite.'

'And if you assure to everybody the means of support without working, nobody will do anything hard or unpleasant, and there will be a universal softening, a universal decay . . .'

To which the answer is 'Ignatius Loyala was very soft and decadent, wasn't he? And the softness and decadence of Oliver Cromwell was, of course, a byword. Historians have never been able to make up their minds whether George Washington was softer and more decadent than the Duke of Wellington. As for the softness and decadence of Queen Victoria . . .'

To suggest that an independent income invariably, or even usually, deters its owner from doing hard, unpleasant work is to be guilty of the most monstrous libel on human nature.

The artists and the writers may not argue quite so foolishly as the economists and the moralists, but one acid but agreeable writer to whom I showed this passage said:

'You seriously alarm me. If your dream came true at least two million people in this country would become novelists. And speaking as a book-reviewer . . .'

'Speaking as a book-reviewer, wouldn't you agree that the great majority of bad novels are written for money?'

'Naturally.'

'And therefore, if there was no need to write for money, the great majority of bad novels wouldn't be written?'

Economic independence would not increase the output of bad art. It would decrease it. And by giving a real equality of education and opportunity it would remove the eternal reproach of those 'mute inglorious Miltons', the very possibility of whose existence is enough to make any decent educated man ashamed of himself.

I am belabouring this point because I am convinced that the 'work-for-the-sake-of-working' doctrine is, in the Age of the Machine, a cruel illusion that is keeping us from the truth. It was exposed, of course, by Christ, in the immortal words 'Mary has chosen that good part'. To many fine, hard-working women those words have always been a stumbling block. They have said to themselves, 'But Martha, after all, was doing her duty. If it weren't for the Marthas of the world, the dishes would never get washed up, the beds would never be made, and the children would always be late for school'.

It is a completely reasonable retort. But Christ (once more), turns everything upside down — even reason itself. And Christ saw how too slavish an attention to duty can sour the soul, how too arduous a service to the household gods can, in the end, draw women away from the service of the only God. The sweeping of rooms is not as vital as the sweeping of the soul. 'An intolerable remark,' some women will say. Perhaps it is. It may suggest a slattern who lolls in a chair, fingering a rosary, while the dust collects in the corners, and the dirt in the kitchen. But this is, really, a cruel interpretation of it. It is certainly not the interpretation of Christ.

XI

Our vision of the Age of Leisure has been obscured by the figures of those materialists whom we evoked, in the interests of honesty.

But it is not difficult to recapture. For in all essentials it is here already. The table is spread. We could sit down and feast — if only we would say grace. In every material thing we have won. It is only in the things of the spirit that we are still defeated. And as a result, Time, for millions of embittered men and women, is a thing to be killed, instead of a thing to be gloriously lived.

Time! It would have a different meaning in that age. At last, for the great majority of mankind, there would be time for dreams. Time to watch the unfolding of the leaves, from the first bud to the last, time to watch their fading, from the first speck of gold to the final fall, time to ponder the significance, which is woven in these branches, of birth and life and death. There would be time for so many things that are lovely and so many things that are strange. Not always, then, would we have to breast the wave. On the water's edge we could linger, while the waves surged towards us, and we would see that each wave had been moulded by a master hand, to give to us a moment of beauty, a moment in which a lovely shape was born of water, with silver wings of spray — an eternal moment, for us alone created.

For then, so many designs which had hitherto been dark to us would emerge from the tapestry of life. There would be a noble rhythm in the seasons and a perfect pattern in the stars. All the meaningless discords of this life would resolve into lovely harmonies. And there would be time, at last, to listen to God. To hear a voice in the wind that is not of this world and an echo from far distances, a whisper that comes from no human lips. He would be there in the silence and in the music, in the empty field at dusk and the full orchestra in the glittering lights, when flute and harp and violin, in a glorious chorus, are celebrating His majesty.

XII

'Very pretty,' snaps the cynic. 'All this through the power of money.'

No.

All this through the power of Christ.

For without the revelation of the spirit, the release from want is nothing. It is merely an escape from a small prison, in which the walls are painted grey, to a large prison, in which the walls are painted gold.

'In that case, why bother?' sneers the cynic. 'If money means nothing, why don't you Christians forget about it? Why think about this life at all?'

We think about it because Christ thought about it. We think about it because we are human and because Christ was human. And being human, he knew our weaknesses, our petty struggles, he knew the barriers which we set between ourselves and the light.

We think about it, in fact, because we are not damned fools.

And on those two words I would end. They are addressed to the orthodox, rationalist financiers.

Damned.

Fools.

And from neither the adjective nor the substantive can they escape, without his help.

CHAPTER V

THE BELLS ARE RINGING

I

As I sit down to write this final chapter, on a dark and stormy evening, the church bells are ringing for evensong. They are fine old bells, and if you were to clamber up the steep stairs to the belfry, taper in hand, you would see that the two earliest date from 1585, and are chiselled with the inscription — Come, come, and preay . . .

For three hundred and fifty years, in fair weather and in foul, those bells have echoed through the valley, and there was a time when people heard them gladly, because they knew that the bells were praising a God who was, indeed, a very present help in trouble. But that was long ago, when the great oaks on the hill were only tiny saplings. To-day, the people find the bells rather a bore. Villagers whose houses lie near the church complain that the noise wakes up their babies, or gives them a headache. And very few people come and pray.

It is in the hope that I may make a few people hear the call of those bells that I have written this book.

II

It has been a strange book to write, because, when I began, I did not know where I should end. And now that I have ended, I have a feeling that the curtain is rising, rather than falling — rising on to a new life. But the drama which remains to be played, can only be played in secret, between the author and his Maker.

Meanwhile I should like, if you will allow me, to answer a few criticisms which may be made of this book, not with the idea of scoring off imaginary opponents but in the earnest hope that I may make clear a few points which may be misunderstood.

The most obvious criticism which the intelligent parson will make is that I have spent too much time in attempting to prove intellectually what can only be proved by the spirit. This is a reasonable, but, I believe, mistaken comment. It ignores the fact that there are tens of thousands of bright and agreeable young people in every 'Christian' country who do not even *try* to 'believe in' Christ, and would regard it as positively eccentric to do so. They would as soon 'believe in' Father Christmas. They have no particular foundations for their scepticism — they certainly haven't made a careful study of the documents, and most of them would be completely floored if you asked them to name a single passage in the gospels which can legitimately be regarded as faked. All they can say is, vaguely, that 'obviously the whole thing's impossible', and they leave it at that.

It was for this reason that I spent so much time on the purely historical aspect of Christianity, because I first guessed, and later knew, that the man who has even for one second 'believed in' Christ can never be quite the same again. Of course you cannot 'prove' the power of Faith, any more than you can 'prove' the beauty of a sunset. But before you can even attempt to discuss Faith you must lead your reader to believe that the thing is, to say the least of it, possible. Otherwise you will be in the position of a man who tries to prove the beauty of the aforesaid sunset to an audience who is firmly convinced that there is no such thing as a sun.

Another criticism which the intelligent parson may make is that I have been unnecessarily 'obvious' in emphasizing the *desirability* of Faith. 'Surely,' he may say, 'you could have taken that for granted?' I do not agree — at least, as far as the younger generations are concerned. The two young moderns whom I quoted from Nöel Coward's comedy *Private Lives* were perfectly satisfied to think that the best they could hope for, after death, was a sort of 'gloomy merging into everything'. At least, they *thought* they were satisfied. Subconsciously, of course, they were desperately unhappy and tortured by ennui, for ennui is the only taste of infinity which the Rationalist will ever permit himself. As a result of this spiritual emptiness and malaise the two principal characters in the play behaved like idiots. After all, if you believe that life is a tale told by an idiot you have every inducement to behave like an idiot yourself. No, I do not think that I wasted time in emphasizing the desirability of Faith. The young people of to-day do desire it, but the majority of them do not *know* that they desire it, which is the reason for a great deal of the world's misery and hate.

III

The tragedy of modern youth's refusal to obey the call of the bells — *Come, come and pray* — lies in the fact that Europe to-day is, perhaps, more widely and deeply religious than ever before. Religious, mark you, not Christian. It should be evident, by now, to the most prejudiced of observers, that the various Youth Movements which have sprung up in passionate support of Europe's dictatorships are religious movements, and nothing else, and that the worship of the dictator, whoever he may be, is a religious worship, with the dictator supplying the place of the Messiah. Youth must have something to worship and the young men who click their heels and cry 'Heil' or 'Duce' or whatever it may be, are, in my opinion, less spiritually degenerate than the young men who drift about loving nothing but themselves and yawning about 'gloomy mergings'.

But though I am not among those who foam at the mouth at the mention of the word 'dictator' — (since the dictators themselves are the inevitable outcome of the selfishness of the post-war settlements, in which we played a predominant part) — there can be, for me, no dictator but Christ, and it is to that end that I shall work — with God knows how many pitiful shortcomings, evasions, and cowardices — for the rest of my life. For Christ has the only answer to the world's problems to-day.

It is necessary to repeat this, over and over again, even at the risk of boring you.

But it isn't boring, if you would only realize that it is true! There *is* no economic problem, no racial problem, no sexual problem, no unemployment problem, no war problem. These 'problems' are myths, ugly phantoms created by minds that are not washed with the spirit of Christ, absurd chimerae that could only flourish in deserts across which the shadow of the cross has never fallen. I know that our lives have no 'problems' as long as we trust in Christ, and the fact that my own life is full of problems at the moment is only a proof of the distance that I still have to travel before reaching perfection. Maybe, I shall never reach it. But at least (to recapture the mood with which our little chapter began) I have 'heard the bells'. And once a man has heard them, they will ring through his mind till the last, and will be caught up and blended in a strange spiritual communion with the final bell that tolls his passing from this world.

I V

To the second part of this book, i.e. the application of revolutionary Christianity to some of the world's greatest problems, I imagine that the principal objection will be that though the ideal is magnificent, it is incapable of realization. If that objection is valid then, of course, we are already, to all intents and purposes, in our graves, and nothing remains to be done except the formality of shovelling earth over our useless carcasses — if there is anybody left to shovel it. However, I do not believe that the objection is valid. The inspiration of movements such as the Oxford Group is evidence to the contrary. They came at the darkest hour — an hour so dark that you could hardly see the gleam of light on their flags as they marched over the dim horizon. But now the light is gathering round them, and their song is echoing round the world.

But it is not through any 'movement', or 'group', or 'revival' that a man is able to speak with assurance of the living Christ, but through the promptings of his own heart. And my own experience is so overwhelmingly convincing that I cannot rest until I have passed it on.

Surely it is *something* for a writer who, at the risk of sounding quite insufferable, can describe himself as a successful man of the world, to state, with bedrock honesty, that he would rather lose every material thing he possesses than his belief in the living presence of Christ? Surely that means *something*? Of course, you may say, all this is a 'stunt', in which case no contempt could be too bitter. But it is not a 'stunt', nor a 'mood'. It is the one true thing I know, that rather than lose my faith in Christ I would give up every material thing.

V

I had meant this chapter to be a summary of the whole book. To be absolutely honest, I had meant to be rather clever in it. But now that the bells have stopped ringing, and darkness is falling over the garden, such a desire seems foolish and a little pitiable. All I want, now, is to tell the truth, and to try to help one or two people.

For the last few minutes, I have been speaking only to the younger generation. But there is one woman who is old, who means more to me than she will ever know, who will perhaps listen to these last words.

She has had a tortured life. She has had to fight, and fight again. And in a sense, she has conquered. At least, through her efforts, through her innate purity and her magnificent courage, she has kept her family together, and has averted the many disasters which might have befallen it. But all these years she has fought by 'instinct', by the light of the God that is in her. She has not really been comforted by God. She has not heard Him speak. She has not *known* that Christ has a message for her. A message which he could give her to-day, if she would only ask.

A plague on this third person singular! I am writing, now, for one woman, who will understand. And so instead of 'she' I will say 'you'.

I want *you*, then (and you will know whom I mean) to realize that if you will only knock, it will be opened unto you. Your sorrow will no longer seem a thing that you must bear yourself. It will be something that you can give, quite literally, to Christ. He is waiting to take it from you — holding out his arms. That is the miraculous significance of the lovely phrase, 'the everlasting arms' of God, and it is echoed in Christ's own words, 'Let not your heart be troubled, neither let it be afraid'.

But as I said before, you must believe. And having believed, you must pray, until the Holy Spirit becomes to you a living voice.

I will tell you some of the things that will happen, if you do.

VI

You will lose your fear of death.

Did you start when you read that? You thought that nobody realized this fear of yours? Well, I realized it.

Love sharpens one's eyes, and many times, in plaintive little sentences, you have betrayed yourself to me.

'Mrs. X is so wonderful,' you have said. 'She will be eighty next month, but she still goes out by herself, and I saw her almost *running* along the street this morning.'

'Yes, she's wonderful.'

And I watch you, after you have spoken, and I know what you are thinking. 'I am old,' you are saying to yourself. 'I may have ten years more ... ten winters, ten summers, ten springs. I needn't worry yet ...'

And then, several times, you have said to me, 'They say that people who reach the age of seventy often have a new lease of life'.

And again I have watched you, and again I have known what was passing through your mind. 'I have passed the danger stage,' you say to yourself. 'I may live till 1946. I need not think of . . . it . . . not yet.'

You are a woman of superlative courage, but you are haunted by this neurosis. For there is poetry in you, and for all of us in whose veins that sweet poison lingers, the transience of earthly things is made more poignant. More swiftly, for us, runs the thin sunlight over the autumn fields, more urgently do we feel that the evenings are drawing in, more desperately do we desire the last few hours of daylight, in which we can walk abroad and see branches that dance darkly across the sky, and hear the last farewell of the birds. There is a savour of frost in the air, as I write . . . winter is on the way . . . the faces of the leaves are flushed before their fall. And I know that you, wherever you may be, will be feeling that frost, too, and that it will chill your spirit as well as your body. And my love for you makes this knowledge bitter.

For the frost is your friend — with the aid of God. Death is your friend — with the aid of Christ. And by death, I mean no ultimate surrender, no despairing sigh, no flutter of lids over tired eyes that can no longer bear the cruel day. For by the love of Christ, the surrender becomes a triumph, the sigh is turned to a song, and the eyes that close are at last the eyes that open.

If I could hold your hands, now at this moment, I believe I could give you that revelation. I cannot do so. I can only write on. . . .

VII

It is dark outside in the garden, and the bells have stopped.

Eight o'clock on an October evening. There are only a few roses left. But there is a drift of autumn crocuses under the old damson tree. And the sweet brier is aflame with scarlet berries. There are plenty of days ahead, in the garden, even now.

But we must not think of it, like that. You and I, who are bound by love, even though our lips may often falter, and though the ridiculous nervous twitch which we call 'humour' may often jerk us away from the true expression of ourselves — you and I must not accept this shabby philosophy, must not try to comfort ourselves with the calendar.

Think of it! That is what millions of people are doing! They are drawing the thin leaves of the calendar about them, saying to themselves, 'I have nearly ten more years ... that means so many thousand leaves ... let me cling to them, and may life tear them slowly for me!' But life does not tear them slowly. Life tears them faster and faster ... so fast in the end, that you have not time to read the little mottoes that are written on them.

And all the time, Christ is waiting for you. Make no mistake about it. He is there — looking over your shoulder. He is saying: 'Let not your heart be troubled, neither let it be afraid.'

One day, I believe, you will hear those words. Not through me, but through him. Then you will turn, and look into his eyes. And you will understand.

And so, though the bells are no longer ringing, and though the garden is shrouded in silence, I pray that you may hear them echoing through your heart, as they are echoing through mine, with their eternal message — Come, Come, and Preay. . . .